Lost Restaurants
OF
FAIRFIELD

PATTI WOODS

AMERICAN PALATE

Published by American Palate
A Division of The History Press
Charleston, SC
www.historypress.net

Copyright © 2015 by Patti Woods
All rights reserved

First published 2015

Manufactured in the United States

ISBN 978.1.46711.803.3

Library of Congress Control Number: 2015950740

CONTENTS

ACKNOWLEDGEMENTS

When acquisitions editor Tabitha Dulla came to me with the idea for this book, I instantly fell in love with the project. It combined three of my passions: Fairfield, restaurants and history. I'm grateful that she approached me and helped make the project a reality. Acquisitions editor Karmen Cook has been a wonderful support through this whole process. Thank you both for all your hard work.

I talked to countless people about their memories of Fairfield's lost restaurants. They willingly offered their stories and photographs and shared joyful memories. To the family, friends and even complete strangers who offered the use of their photographs and ephemera, I thank you from the bottom of my heart.

This book wouldn't have been possible without social media. Two Facebook pages in particular were my go-to resources when I needed answers. Thank you to all the members of "Life in Fairfield & Westport"; your memories and stories helped immensely. Beth Bilyard, Whitney Mercurio and Ken Bullard, thank you for allowing me to constantly post on your page. And to the "Fairdalers" at "You Grew Up in the Town of Fairfield, CT, pre-1990," your input was invaluable. Paul Brundage and Sandy Werthmann, I appreciate all your help.

To Elizabeth Rose and Ellen O'Meara at the Fairfield Museum and History Center, your time and willingness to assist in this venture are so appreciated. Thank you Heather-Marie Montilla and all the folks at the Pequot Library who allowed access to the library's resources.

ACKNOWLEDGEMENTS

It goes without saying that a project like this couldn't be accomplished without the support and encouragement from family and friends. Thank you to John Schwing, editor extraordinaire; I clung to your brilliant advice and reassurance during those dead-end days. Susan Siverson, I knew I could count on you for whatever I needed, whether it was a slice from Mike's or a daily text update. Thank you for always having my back. Thank you Heidi Gamma, your Sunday dinners filled my stomach and my soul; and Nick Gamma, your amazing photography and design skills never fail to impress me. Kara Canney—the Trumbull children's librarian who brought me blueberry tea and "shushed" the noisy patrons—you rock. Amy Okrepkie, your flexibility and encouragement at my day job made the process so much easier—not to mention the best massages around. To all of the members of the Gaelic American Club who let me interrupt your dinner to talk restaurants, I raise my glass to you.

To my husband, Brian, and son, Henri, your patience and understanding during this time haven't gone unnoticed. I couldn't ask for a better cheering section. You are my world.

Lastly, thank you to my parents. My mother, Joan Woods, unfailingly told everyone she met about this project and scouted out potential resources—you truly are the world's best mom. My father, George Woods, passed away during the writing of this book. He shared with me the subtle joy that comes from a perfect turkey club and a glass of unsweetened iced tea. We always ordered the same thing at restaurants. I dedicate this book to him.

$\P$NTRODUCTION

To begin with, let me say: this is not a concise history of Fairfield's gastronomic past. To attempt to cover each and every eatery that once operated in town would be a herculean task. If it could be accomplished, this book would then double as a door stop. There have just been too many food and drink establishments in the town's 375-year history to try to chronicle with any hope of 100 percent accuracy. Instead, this book contains the memories, stories and photos of a sampling of the town's most beloved restaurants. Some of the research came from old newspaper articles and saved bits of ephemera, but most of it came from oral histories—stories that have been passed down through the generations of people who owned, worked and patronized the town's businesses. Some of these lost restaurants are memorialized only in the old telephone directories, their tales having been forgotten over the years. Often, nothing exists but a simple text ad, like the one for Lolly's from a 1939 directory that reads, "Formerly the Red Barn Tavern, 43 Unquowa Road. Sandwiches—Hot Meats. Ruppert's Beer, Ballantine's Ale. Newly Redecorated and Remodeled. Lolly Bogucki, Proprietor." One can only imagine Bogucki behind the bar wearing a white apron and serving up simple corned beef sandwiches with cold pints of ale.

Today, dining out is a regular occurrence for most families. But fifty years ago, the restaurant scene was different. When interviewing people for this book, I was told countless times, "We didn't go out to dinner that often." Going out to a restaurant was a rare and special occasion. The importance of such opportunities was enough to create lasting memories of dressing up and being on one's best behavior, hands folded politely on the white tablecloth.

For more recent generations, though, dining out is a regular part of daily life. These stories consisted of weekly visits to the same restaurant, the same bar stool, the same table and the same waiter. For them, the memories of lost restaurants bring about a sort of nostalgia comparable to thinking of one's childhood home. These restaurants were places of familiarity, comfort and acceptance. In interviewing people for the chapter on bars, I was told on numerous occasions that certain bars were "just like Cheers—a place where everybody knew your name."

Part of the fun—and frustration—in researching this book was coming across restaurants I'd never even heard of. The first time someone mentioned the Donald Duck, I thought they were kidding. The second time, my ears perked up. By the third mention, I was on the hunt. There were no articles or photos to be found anywhere, just vague recollections from people of an older generation. I finally uncovered an ad from an old directory that said, "After the Minstrel, visit the Donald Duck Restaurant, 236 King's Highway. Fine Foods—Finest Liquors—Italian Spaghetti—Mixed Drinks—Beer—Wine. Open until 3 a.m." Its existence was confirmed.

Other times, there were restaurants that plenty of people had heard of or been to, but there was no documentation to be found. I desperately wanted to find an article, a menu, anything from the Thunderbird, the Rocket or the Roadside Inn, but I ended my searches empty-handed. One can only surmise that the historians of the past had no idea what a food-centric culture we would become. How could they ever have imagined that people would make a hobby out of reading cookbooks and actually watching people create meals on television? Surely they couldn't imagine a culture so fascinated by food that the term "foodie" would become part of the twentieth-first-century lexicon. So it's only natural that they wouldn't have considered saving menus, placemats or recipes from local restaurants. Who would ever have an interest in such mundane things?

As it turns out, we the people of the twenty-first century do. We love to debate and discuss ideas, and the food world offers us plenty of opportunity. Veganism versus paleo, locavorism versus GMOs, comfort food versus haute cuisine—there is no end to the passionate analyses conducted by gastronomes. But even those who don't consider themselves "foodies" were willing to enthusiastically reminisce about Fairfield's favorite haunts. Part of the fun in creating this book was meeting people of all ages and backgrounds who willingly and joyfully shared their memories. While local politics and generational differences may separate people, a common love and nostalgia for our lost restaurants brings us together. The mere mention of a lost restaurant—say Howard Johnson's or Breakaway—would spur enthusiastic conversations about favorite bartenders, cranky waitresses and high school hijinks.

It's been interesting to look at Fairfield's history through the eyes—or perhaps more accurately the stomachs—of the different generations. Today you'd be hard-pressed to find a restaurant that didn't offer a selection of salads, but go back to the 1940s and you won't find a kale salad on the menu. Today health is the driving force in deciding what to eat, whereas even twenty years ago, menus were resplendent with steaks, burgers and heavy sauces. Surprisingly, the town's proximity to the water has rarely factored into the restaurant scene. One would expect a plethora of seafood dishes on local menus when, in fact, this seems to be the one category that has been consistently lacking.

Without a doubt, transportation played a huge role in the Fairfield scene. In 1894, the first trolley began doing runs from Bridgeport to Southport. This allowed people the freedom to visit nearby towns and, in turn, sample different restaurants. With the introduction of the automobile in the early 1900s, the pastime of the day was to drive from town to town, stopping at tea houses and small cafés along the way. It's charming to imagine motorcars full of people stopping to have tea and sandwiches at the Old Academy Tea Room and then continuing on their journeys up the coast. When the section of the Merritt Parkway from Norwalk to Trumbull opened in 1939, travel to Fairfield was easier and more convenient, even from towns farther afield. In 1958, when the Fairfield County section of the Connecticut Turnpike opened, access to all parts of town was now available. This meant more opportunities for restaurants in Fairfield to achieve huge levels of success.

While not strictly restaurants, I've included a chapter on Fairfield's taverns, saloons and bars. Much of the town's identity was defined by the local watering holes. Fairfield had a surprisingly colorful relationship with alcohol. Early colonial laws were strict, and the temperance movement was fierce, yet Fairfielders always managed to find a way to support a local tavern. In the late 1800s, Southport's saloons took on an almost Wild West feel, with more than a few reports of injuries and gun fights, a surprising juxtaposition to the village today. In the first half of twentieth century, Fairfield's bars—from coastal establishments like Beachside, Davie's, Surfside and the Nautilus to beer and shot places like Al's and the Driftwood—were places where the locals gathered to share friendship, gossip and the occasional bar fight. Later, with a burgeoning interest in wine and the invention of frozen cocktails, the town's bar scene took on a more sophisticated note. Without a doubt, Fairfield's social scene has always revolved around the tap.

I've also included bakeries and ice cream parlors in this book. From as early as the nineteenth century, it is clear that Fairfielders loved their sweets. Whether it was a pastry from Hall's Home Made Bakery or an ice cream purchased after a trolley ride into Southport, locals had ways of satisfying their sweet tooth.

My hope is that this book spurs fun and lively conversation about Fairfield's culinary past. This written history is just the start; your personal stories and memories complete the picture. Use this book as a tool. Ask your friends what they remember, what their favorite restaurant was and what dish they really wish they could have just one more time. You might be surprised just how long the conversation lasts.

1

ỲE OLDE ỲAVERNS AND ỲNNS

Dining in Colonial Fairfield

The most logical place to begin is with a look at Fairfield's colonial past. In recent decades, there have been amazing restaurants in Fairfield that specialize in burgers and pizza and sushi. There have been greasy spoon diners and fancy white tablecloth restaurants. But before all of that, taverns (where one could get an alcoholic drink) and ordinaries (which offered meals) catered to locals and travelers.

In 1644, the Colonial Records of Connecticut ordered "one sufficient inhabitant" in each town to keep an ordinary, since "strangers were straitened" for want of a place of public entertainment."[1] In other words, every town was required to have at least one place where travelers could get a bite to eat and relax after traveling all day on roads that were amazingly even more treacherous than I-95 today.

In 1780, Samuel Penfield built the Sun Tavern. Any good Fairfielder knows of the Sun Tavern, where "yes," people will say with a knowing chuckle, "Washington really did stay." We know this because of his diaries. In an entry dated October 16, 1789, Washington wrote, "From hence [Norwalk] to Fairfield where we dined and lodged is 12 miles; and part of it is very rough road, but not equal to that thro' horse neck." A month later, on a return trip, he wrote, "Set out about sunrise, and took the upper road to Milford, it being shorter than the lower one through West Haven. Breakfasted in the former. Baited at Fairfield and dined and lodged at Majr. Marvins."[2] When he says he baited, he didn't mean fishing. In those days, baited meant having a small meal. His diaries don't tell us exactly what he ate (clearly he wasn't as hip to journaling about the food scene as Thomas Jefferson was), but it's fun to imagine.

One of Fairfield's first dining establishments, the Sun Tavern is famous for having had George Washington as a guest. *Courtesy of the author.*

Given Fairfield's proximity to the water and Washington's fondness for fish, it seems safe to assume that there was some sort of seafood on the menu. Oysters and clams were plentiful, and they were the sources of local legends. In a report by local historian William Lee, he wrote, "The story goes that Ben Franklin walked in the front door and the tavern was filled to the brim. He looked to the right and to the left; he looked out the door and he finally said to one of his attendants that he was delighted to be in Fairfield. Franklin said that he was especially delighted to be at the Sun Tavern because there was such an abundance of seafood—more than he had ever seen any place in his life. So much, in fact, that they were serving oysters to horses in the stable. With that, there was a scramble of people for the door to have a look in the stable. And Ben went over and took a seat."[3]

We do know that Washington had false teeth (made of bone, not wood, as legend would have it), and given the rudimentary dental practices of the day and the absence of denture cream, one would imagine that his choppers weren't as functional as he would've liked. Knowing that, perhaps soft foods were on the menu—applesauce or maybe mashed vegetables? In its early beginnings, Fairfield was an agricultural town. Squash, beans and corn were major crops, so perhaps Washington enjoyed some succotash or Indian pudding.

According to one article, "Folks still exist who have been told tales of luscious pies, cakes and bread which used to come from [the] oven within memory of those, now passed on, who remembered seeing batches taken from this oven on baking days."[4] In addition, there was a brick wine vault in the cellar where wines and liquors were stored.

It might be surprising to note that the president had a bit of a sweet tooth. "Washington paid a good amount of money for ice cream, though it may have been more custard-like," said Walter Matis, program and volunteer coordinator for the Fairfield Museum and History Center.

In addition to Washington's diaries, there have also been stories of his visit passed down through the generations. One article from the early twentieth century recalls such a remembrance. "Not long ago lived a woman whose mother had seen the president seated at a table in the tavern. She was but a little girl, and had to stand on tiptoe to peer over the window ledge in order to see this greatest man of his country. The common and tavern yard were filled with grownups from all around the country side and hills, drawn there by word that President Washington was coming to town."[5] The scene sounded quite similar to that when President Ronald Reagan visited the town green in 1984 and visitors clogged the adjoining streets to get a glimpse of him.

In 1818, the tavern became a private residence, but much of the original architecture remained. "The old kitchen, where tavern keepers made preparations for guests, retained much of its ancient atmosphere down through generations, in spite of modern additions more suitable to a housewife's use. The big crane, dangling heavy chains, pothooks and trammels of old tavern days, rests in obscurity behind a great fireboard, which is held in place by wooden buttons."

After the Sun Tavern closed, the men of the town were anxious to have a new meeting place. A group got together and decided to nominate Captain Abraham Benson as the keeper. They said, "The subscribers being desirous that a public Inn should be established in the village of Fairfield for the entertainment of travelers which shall be exempt from the vices of intemperance and tavern haunting, with neat and ample accommodations for horses and carriages and guests, being assured by Captain Benson that he will keep a house of that character, they recommend him to the proper board to be nominated for that purpose."[6]

DISTINGUISHED GUESTS

The building, facing west down the Old Post Road, stood on the site of a house owned by General Elijah Abel, deputy for Fairfield.[7] "The old Benson tavern was a regular stopping point for the stage. Horses were changed at

Stamford, and the coaches arrived at the inn in time for supper. The list of distinguished guests who have stopped here, during the coaching era, is long and impressive. It includes Fanny Kemble, Edwin Booth, Aaron Burr, Daniel Webster, Macready and General Jackson."[8]

Another tavern facing the green was Bulkley's tavern, "a two-story house with a large ell on the west and a one-story wing on the right." Surprisingly, when the town was burned in 1779, the tavern was somehow spared (aside from some shattered window glass and a chimney that was demolished by a cannonball). The tavern then became the headquarters for General Tryon. The keeper of the inn was Joseph Bulkley, who also owned a store a short distance away. At one point, thieves broke into the store and stole all the dry goods. After that, Bulkley gave up shopkeeping and connected the store to the tavern's bar room, using it as a dining room. Later, the tavern was renamed Hull's, "with the sign of a black horse."[9] It was known for its entertainment, and there were dances once a month at which visitors were served wine and plum cake. Lawyers from Litchfield and other communities came to Fairfield to attend court and stopped at Hull's tavern for food.[10] The tavern also contained the offices of Fairfield's first newspaper, the *Fairfield Gazette*, which began publishing in 1786.[11] It certainly must have been convenient for Bulkley and his other newspapermen—Stephen Miller and Francis Forgue Jr.—to indulge in a pint of ale after deadline. On July 29, 1868, Reverend Samuel Nichols bought the building and used it for storage. Eventually, the tavern fell into disrepair, and in 1912, it was struck by lightning and burned.[12]

While tavern keeping may have been largely a man's occupation, there was at least one exception. In 1806, when Molly Pike became widowed, she converted her Southport house into an inn in order to support herself and her fifteen children. The Molly Pike Tavern stood across from Southport Harbor for three decades before it burned in 1894.

In addition to providing lodging and food for travelers, the local inns and taverns were places of great celebration. Bulkley kept notes in his diaries about the local parties. He wrote of a "Negro Frolic," which lasted for two days, and an Oyster Frolic. "With their sanded floors, oak tables, benches around the room, applejack and 'good old brown October ale' on tap, and 'good stuff' in the basement, these establishments could always find a fiddler—Moses Sturges was a favorite—and put on a dance."[13] Clearly taverns enlivened early colonial life.

2
ŦEETOTALERS AND ŦIPPLERS

Fairfield's Bar Scene

Fairfield was quick to establish laws pertaining to the use of alcohol. As far back as the 1630s, there were rules put in place to restrict the sale of liquor. These rules cited that "no person should sell wine, liquor or strong water in any place, without a license from the particular court, or from two magistrates." And so began Connecticut's rigorous liquor license process. Furthermore, "to prevent the abuse of wine and strong water, it was ordered: 'That no inhabitant in any town should continue in a tavern or victualizing house in the town in which he lived more than half an hour at a time, drinking wine, beer, or hot water.'"[14] So much for the idea of happy hour.

Over the years, libations came in and out of favor. In 1829, the Fairfield Temperance Society began holding monthly meetings. "The members all agreed to abstain from the use of alcoholic beverages and to urge others to do likewise; they believed 'that the use of intoxicating liquors is, for persons in health, not only unnecessary, but hurtful and that the practice is the cause of forming intemperate appetites and habits.'"[15]

Not everyone was a teetotaler, however. Southport, in particular, had its share of those who liked to imbibe. "The waterfront area was a spirited place, abutting Main Street's post office and stores," wrote V. Louise Higgins in the *Southport Packet*.[16] "There the ladies saw more public drunkenness than they liked, to their mind too often in the form of a tipsy seaman whose rolling gait ashore did not suggest to them someone just off a romantic quarterdeck. As temperance movements gathered strength in the latter part of the 19th century, the focal point of the Southport struggle between the wets and the drys became the harborfront stores." There were two contingents: those who objected entirely to alcohol and the moderates who saw the value in saloons as a sort of social club. Liquor licenses were routinely applied for and denied. In July 1889, however, a liquor permit was given to the town drugstore. The temperance faction were unhappy, and vandalism and protests occurred. For four years, liquor permits continued to be denied. Then, in April 1893, Fred Mills was granted a license for a saloon in a new building. The dry town was slowly becoming damp.

The teetotalers tried to provide an alternative to the local saloons. On Halloween 1901, Reverend Edmund Guilbert, rector of Trinity Episcopal Church in Southport, undertook an experimental venture. He rented out a storefront and created the Hollywood Inn. William C. Jennings acted as the manager, and the inn was open every day except Sunday from 2:00 to 10:00 p.m. There, men could play checkers and chess and enjoy coffee and cake and the occasional dinner. It was glaringly alcohol free. The inn was the only place in town where "young men can spend an evening attended with all the safeguards of home, and without the temptation of sale of whiskey or beer."[17]

The Hollywood Inn was well attended, but that didn't seem to affect Southport's saloons. In fact, things were just starting to get a little out of hand.

SOUTHPORT: THE WILD WEST

Take, for example, the story of an argument turned violent. In 1911, a fight occurred at the Round House Café, which was located opposite what is now the junction of the Boston Post Road and the Connecticut Turnpike. According to a newspaper report, Julius Cheeseman was drinking at the bar alone when he was confronted by three men. An argument ensued, and the men were told to take it outside. Fists started to fly, and one of the three drew out a knife and cut Cheeseman over the eye.[18] The proprietor of the Round House, Stephen Royak, wrote a letter to the newspaper saying that no such attack occurred and that it was maliciously intended to hurt his business.[19]

Then there was Casper Schick, a saloon owner who found himself in the news more than once. His café was located at Ash Creek in Southport. In 1911, he was arrested, charged with illegally delivering a case of beer to Westport, where he didn't have a license.[20] At the time, he was only allowed to sell beer within the confines of Southport.

From 1909 to 1912, Casper Schick operated a saloon in Southport. *Left to right*: Prince, a Southport dog; Albert Pike; Southport oyster boat captain; Jack Johnston, bartender; unidentified customer; Carl Schick, age seven; Casper Schick, owner; Chris Schick, age five; and two unidentified Southporters. *Courtesy of the Fairfield Museum and History Center.*

In 1913, with business presumably booming, Schick then went on to purchase a saloon and restaurant located at 1148 Main Street in Bridgeport from John F. Sullivan for $9,300. Sullivan sold the business after he was shot in the abdomen by a waiter named Bruno, who remained at large.[21]

The local newspaper spared no drama when it reported on a fight that took place at Schick's tavern in Fairfield. "Modern warfare with its starshells and hand-to-hand combats in the trenches was emulated on a small scale recently in Fairfield, and yesterday the details of the struggle were told in Judge Bacon Wakeman's town court."[22] The article tells of an argument between three Polish-speaking men and Bridgeport resident Andrew Soss. The men had a heated debate about the Allies' involvement in the war and then Soss vanished. Soss allegedly returned with a rifle and a friend.

"Witnesses declare that there was a flash of light, followed by a dull thud. There was a second flash of light, a whang and another dull thud, continued by at least two more flashes and thuds, followed by groans. The light disappeared and Soss was seen no more. Half an hour later Schick's saloon took the form of an improvised field hospital."[23] Ultimately, Soss was found guilty and fined five dollars and served ten days in jail.

Meanwhile, on Water Street, Christian Rist had owned a saloon for thirty years. In what today would certainly be a controversial move, Rist's liquor license was suddenly revoked. "There has never been any complaint against Rist personally," the newspaper reported, "but when the Wakeman Memorial home was erected near the saloon a short time ago a remonstrance was filed against Rist on the ground that the location was unsuitable."[24] So much for first come first served. The article stated the obvious: "The loss of his license will be a serious blow to Rist."

Rist wasn't about to sit back and let his license be taken away. He hired Judge Elmore S. Banks to represent him in superior court. Again, it was decided that his license could not be renewed. [25]

When World War I began, rationing, growing and preserving fruits and vegetables and pig farming were encouraged. In the fall of 1917, to further homeland support, Judge Bacon Wakeman opposed granting any licenses for the sale of alcoholic beverages in town.[26] Every year at town elections, the residents would vote whether the town would be wet or dry.[27] One might imagine that election time was particularly stressful for local tavern owners, not knowing if they'd be out of a job the next day.

That year, 433 people sided with Wakeman against licensing, but 554 voted to keep the town's saloons open. The town had its priorities.

One of Southport's longest-standing bars still open today is the Horseshoe Café. It's the place to go for live music and good beer on tap. But before the Horseshoe we know today, there was a different building on the site. In the 1920s, Edward Russell built a blacksmith shop in the center of Southport. In 1933, it was renovated as Russell's Horse Shoe Tavern, and in 1934, in order to serve liquor on Sundays in accordance with the law, it was made into a restaurant. By that time, people were starting to get automobiles, and the villagers of Southport feared that the narrow roads in the center of town were much too dangerous. A petition was created suggesting that Pequot Avenue should be widened. This proposed widening meant that, among other things, the new road would cut right through the Horse Shoe Tavern.[28] Edward Russell was not happy, nor was his son Edward (Ned), who had opened a life insurance and real estate agency in town. His grandson Ned Russell recalled their feelings about the situation:

The original Horse Shoe Restaurant was built in 1933. According to local legend, the bar stools were removed in order to keep women out of the saloon. This photo is dated "post-Prohibition." *Courtesy of the Fairfield Museum and History Center/Pequot Library.*

The initial plan called for the widening to extend the entire length of Pequot Avenue to Southport Beach. There was much opposition which included many residents much more influential and affluent than my father at that time. When the plan was cut back to Center Place, my father was virtually alone in the protest and was bitter over the fact [that] his land was the most affected.[29]

In 1947, the original Horse Shoe restaurant was razed by members of the fire department.[30]

1,500-Foot Law

Interestingly enough, temperance wasn't just a construct of the early twentieth century. In 1962, a strange phenomenon occurred: the Woman's Christian Temperance Union and some of Fairfield's liquor purveyors found themselves on the same side of a local debate.[31] There was a proposal in front of the town planning and zoning committee to abolish the 1,500-foot rule—an ordinance that prohibited the establishment of any liquor outlet within 1,500 feet of another. Some restaurants weren't able to secure liquor permits because of their proximity to other dining establishments that already had licenses. Howard Johnson's was one such restaurant. The nearby Fairfield Inn already was serving drinks. On Tunxis Hill, Richard

The Fairfield Inn offered breakfast, lunch and dinner, as well as a full bar. Nearby, Howard Johnson's was unable to get a liquor permit because of the 1,500-foot rule. *Courtesy of the Fairfield Museum and History Center.*

Stiegler, who owned the A&P supermarket, hoped to put in a package store next door. The only problem was Kuhn's Bar and Grill already had a brisk bar business. The members of the Temperance Union of course would have preferred that all liquor stores and taverns be outlawed, so their protestations of the proposal were understood. But many established restaurateurs felt that it would be unfair to abolish the rule. One liquor store owner was quoted as saying, "This is a legitimate trade. But when you allow these places to spring up one on top of another, you end up with a shanty town." Eventually, the zoning laws did change, as evidenced by Fairfield's bustling and ever-expanding restaurant scene today.

Throughout the history of the town, taverns, saloons, bars—whatever you want to call them—were an integral part of the community. In the twentieth century, small neighborhood bars served as gathering places. "The best thing about a great neighborhood bar is the range of people that go there to unwind and connect at the end of the day," said Christine Sismondo, author of *America Walks Into a Bar: A Spirited History of Taverns and Saloons, Speakeasies and Grog Shops* (Oxford University Press, 2011).[32] "You get everyone from chefs to lawyers and cab drivers to professors and, when the subject turns to current events or the local sports team, nobody's opinion counts more than anyone else's. The bar is a real equalizer and, at the best of them, people check their credentials at the door and try to just relate like normal people for a few hours."

THE BEER AND A SHOT CROWD

Fairfield's downtown had two working-class neighborhood bars that achieved local legendary status. Al's Place and the Driftwood were the protectorates of the pre-yuppie Fairfield. Al's, located on the corner of the Post Road and Thorpe Street, had been a bar since 1935, when it was called Jenning's Grill. The name was then changed to Al's Place when it was bought by Al Jasko Sr. in the 1950s. In August 2000, Christine and Al Boccamazzo bought the café from the estate of Al Jasko's son.[33]

Christine was no stranger to the restaurant business. Her grandparents John and Nellie Galaske owned the Thunderbird Drive-In in Southport. "It was an old-fashioned drive-in with counter service," Boccamazzo recalled. "They had real milkshakes and burgers." She worked there starting when she was thirteen years old until it closed in 1975. Her grandfather had then

The Driftwood was the last of the working-class bars in Fairfield Center. *Courtesy of the Fairfield Museum and History Center.*

bought the property at the corner of Thorpe and Post Road—the site that would become Al's. In 2000, when the business came up for sale, she decided to take it over and clean it up. "We put in a new bar, a new floor, put up a new façade, re-did the bathrooms and expanded it to have live music," she said. Yet the regulars still came. Boccamazzo talked about the "breakfast club"—a group of men who, over the course of forty years, had met daily from 9:00 a.m. to 12:00 p.m. "It was fun," she said. "I still see a lot of them around. They would tell you stories and do crossword puzzles." She said in the afternoon, there was a regular crowd that would play Liar's Poker. In 2005, the Boccamazzos sold Al's to Mark Chandler and Chung Huynh, who owned it for a year. The week of June 19, 2006, was devastating for Fairfield's "beer-and-shot" crowd. Not only did Al's close, but the Driftwood saw its last day as well.

The Driftwood, located at 1612 Post Road, opened in 1967.[34] It was far from fancy. The wood-paneled room had a bar and a few tables. A coat rack was available to hang your jacket, and photos and beer signs lined the walls. Behind the bar, bottles were lined up, along with American flags and a sign that said, "I can only please one person per day. Today is not your day. Tomorrow doesn't look good either." If you wanted a beer or a Canadian Club and water, this might be your place. A glass of wine or a fancy martini? You'd best move along.

Behind the bar, Millie Larsen poured drinks from day one. In the 1950s, she worked down the street as a bartender at Rudy's. She settled into the Driftwood, where her regular patrons called her "Mom." On Sundays, she would cook a buffet, which she would serve up for free to patrons so they wouldn't drink on empty stomachs. It was the kind of place where, instead of playing pool or darts, you'd sit and shoot the breeze. The Driftwood closed on June 23, 2006, the day its liquor license expired. Local newspapers ran articles featuring Larsen.

"One of the things that made this such a good bar was that we did not have that many fist fights," she was quoted as saying in the *Connecticut Post*. "I mean, there were a few, but there was always somebody here who'd break it up."[35]

The loss of Al's Place and the Driftwood was the end of an era for Fairfield. As Clarence Jennings said in an article in the *Connecticut Post*, "All your shot-and-beer drinkers, your working people, your two-, three-, four-dollar people, they're not going to have any place to go, especially with the Driftwood closing and Al's closing. You've got a bunch of kids' bars, but you don't have any man's bars."[36]

SAVE THE SURFSIDE

Today, real estate along the coastline is highly sought after, but that wasn't always the case. In the early twentieth century, small summer cottages (oftentimes simple shacks) lined the streets near the Fairfield beaches. Unlike the year-round community that the area is today, the streets on the shoreline were mostly populated only in the summers. It wasn't until the 1960s when the area started to change to a four-season community. At the end of South Pine Creek Road sat Davie's Restaurant. There, you could walk straight from the beach to a service window and get a hot dog or Sealtest ice cream. In 1961, Joe Sepot, then a twenty-five-year-old entrepreneur, purchased the property. He renamed the business Surfside. "In 1961, I made Surfside into the first beer garden in the state of Connecticut," he said.[37] Beach visitors could still walk up to the window to order hot dogs during the day, but at night, revelers came to drink and listen to live music. "The business was so big, we had to have three squad cars to direct traffic," said Sepot.

Surfside was the only business in this residential section of town, so Sepot had to go to the liquor commission every year to renew his license. "Pine Creek was the worst section of town at the time," he said. "But the property was grandfathered in, so there wasn't anything anyone could do about it."

For sunbathers spending the day at South Pine Creek beach, Davie's offered hot dogs, ice cream and cold beer. *Courtesy of Joseph Sepot.*

After Davie's, the building located at the end of South Pine Creek Road was transformed into the Surfside, one of Connecticut's first beer gardens. *Courtesy of Joseph Sepot.*

But the neighbors certainly tried. Some area residents banded together to create the Pine Creek Area Association, and they attended the hearings in Hartford with the liquor commission. Complaining of "a nightly onslaught of cars, noise, rowdyism, urinating in public and various other public nuisances," the neighbors fought to shut down Surfside.[38] In town, bumper stickers imploring, "Save the Surfside" began appearing on cars. As a result of one hearing, Sepot was ordered to clean up litter around the building, lower the noise level from the music and submit a parking plan.

At another time, the then town health director Dr. H. Patterson Harris Jr. ordered the capacity of the Surfside to be reduced on the grounds that the bar didn't have a sufficient number of toilets.[39]

Yet business remained brisk at Surfside. "We ran bands five nights a week," said Sepot. "We went through five hundred cases of Schaefer a week." Surfside attracted local bands but also up and coming stars such as Otis Blackwell and ShaNaNa. "You know you've got a good band when you have to take the furniture out," Sepot said.

Ultimately, the Surfside wouldn't last. However, its closing wasn't due to neighborhood complaints. It was the change in drinking laws. In 1972, the

Promising a "wild time for all," the Monster Mash was just one of the Surfside's nights of entertainment. *Courtesy of Joseph Sepot.*

Connecticut drinking age was lowered from twenty-one to eighteen. "I sold Surfside because eighteen year olds were drinking and I was babysitting," said Sepot. "I had no interest in that." The bar closed, and in 1983 it was demolished and replaced by Kensie Point condominiums.

The Surfside was just one of the local beach bars. The others included the Sandbar, on the Fairfield/Black Rock border, and the Beachside, located directly across from Penfield Beach and where the New York Giants would hang out. (From 1961 to 1969, they trained at Fairfield University.) At the corner of Reef Road and Fairfield Beach Road stood a run-down, cinderblock bar that was known to just about every eighteen-year-old in town. The Nautilus had a reputation as a cheap bar that didn't always card underage drinkers. Some called it "the Nauseous" and recalled that the floors were always sticky. Pitchers of Genesee were $1.99. "You could leave the Naut and pass out on the beach," recalled one former patron. The bar was divided into two sections: one with a pool table, the other with tables and chairs. The bathrooms are still a source of laughter today. "I remember when they had boarded up one of the bathrooms on the not-pool-table side," said Jen Collison.[40] "A bunch of us were sitting at a table nearby when the door flew open and the unattached toilet and sink fell out. We looked up, startled, but since it was the Naut, we just went back to the beer."

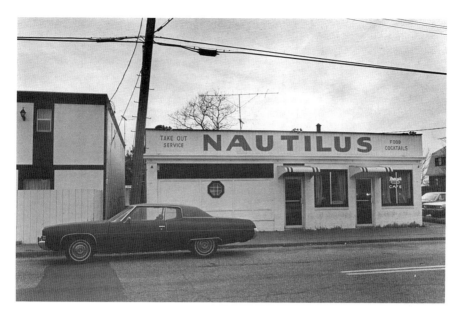

It wasn't much to look at, but the Nautilus's proximity to the beach made it one of the most popular spots in town. *Courtesy of the Fairfield Museum and History Center.*

Mary Beth Ross recalled, "I once told the bartender that the toilet in the restroom was overflowing. He pointed to the decorative life ring on the wall and said, 'Don't worry, we have life preservers.'"[41]

Yet, despite its appearance, the Nautilus was beloved by many. Before it was the Nautilus, it was first Maynard's Reef, a place to get burgers and play pinball after spending hours at the beach. Then it became a bar called Flanagan's and then, in the 1960s, the Nautilus. For a brief time, it was known as Your Brother's Suspenders before it went back to being called the Nautilus. In 1985, the Naut was shut down after the owner, William Gregorio, failed to correct several health, fire and building code violations.[42] Today it is the Seagrape, a bar frequented by Fairfield University students.

A TASTE OF THE TROPICS

In the 1950s, Ellie Simpson lived in Fairfield. For a time, she worked the night shift at the Ess Diner in Southport as a waitress. Then she moved on to the Red Galleon, a seafood restaurant in Westport, where she made a lot of friends and met several celebrities. "People always said, 'You should own your own place.' I took it as bar talk," said Simpson.[43]

But then one day in 1969, Simpson and a friend were driving down the Post Road in Fairfield and saw that Sullivan's Bar at 1599 Post Road was available. (Today this is the location of Quattro Pazzi.) "My friend said, 'Let's go see.' So we went in and met Bessie Sullivan and talked about wanting to own a bar. I had $50 in my pocket," said Simpson. "I had a lot of nerve. Bessie told me, 'If you can bring me $1,000 today, we can talk.'"

Simpson contacted some people who had offered to help her and by the afternoon had culled together the down payment. She partnered with friend Ray Bayus.

The setting was perfect. Simpson had moved to a house on a street just behind the bar, so she would be able to keep an eye on her six children while still running the business.

"The place had to be totally redone," recalled Simpson. "It was just a bar with booths." Simpson decided she wanted to go with a South Seas

The Lotus, with its Hawaiian theme, was owned by Ellie Simpson. Here, she and her business partner, Ray Bayus, entertain a young guest. *Courtesy of Ellie Simpson.*

theme, similar to a restaurant that she frequented in New York. The place was decorated with bamboo and flowers.

"It took us three months, but it was lovely. It was the nicest place in town," she said. The day before opening, Simpson said they needed to come up with a name. "I said, 'What are we going to call this place?' It looks Hawaiian, and I know they make a dish with lotus flowers, so let's call it the Lotus. It sounds classy."

The morning of the grand opening, Simpson said there were men sitting on the guard rail outside waiting for the place to open. The Lotus was off to an auspicious start. Simpson put bowls of macadamia nuts out on the bar and gave out cheap plastic Hawaiian leis. "You wouldn't believe how impressed people were with those."

The specialty drink of the house was called a Suffering Bastard—a mix of passionfruit, rum, and other ingredients—served in a skull-shaped mug. "If you could drink two of those, you could take the mug home," said Simpson.

A week after opening, Simpson brought in a band to play live music. A local trio called the Beachcombers started off playing Hawaiian tunes, but eventually moved on to western music. "They really brought the people in," said Simpson. The band ended up playing seven nights a week.

Simpson loved her customers, and anytime there was an occasion to celebrate, she'd open a bottle of champagne. "Anytime anyone had a birthday or a baby, we'd open a bottle," she said. "It was an eleven-year party."

The best times, though, were the St. Patrick's Day celebrations. Long before most bars ever thought of making a celebration out of the holiday, Simpson was on the cutting edge. "We had green beer, which was silly, but people loved it," said Simpson. "We made giant lobster pots full of corned beef and cabbage. We had Irish dancers, the bagpipers and drummers would go through the bar. It was lots of fun."

Memorial Day presented another big opportunity for the Lotus. The annual parade would travel down the Post Road, and residents would line their lawn chairs out in front of the bar. It may have been before noon, but that didn't stop many people from popping in for a quick beer.

Simpson proved to be a tough cookie when it came to protecting her business. She said she rarely had any trouble from anyone. The one story she offered was the night when one of the players from the New York Giants came in. Occasionally the players, and once even Frank Gifford, came in. One night, one of the players started making a mess, throwing chips around and stomping them into the flower-shaped rug. Simpson threw him out, and he never returned.

John Barnhart recalled spending many nights at the Lotus. "We used to play darts there," he said. "If we got tired of darts, we went across the street to the Driftwood to play cards."[44]

Over the years, Simpson's children helped out at the Lotus. When her daughter turned twenty-one, she worked the bar. Her son Timmy cleaned the bar every morning. Sadly, though, in 1979, her partner Bayus was diagnosed with cancer, and Simpson decided she didn't want to run the bar alone. She decided the Lotus had run its course.

BEER AT THE BUTTON BALL

The Tunxis Hill section of Fairfield had its own local watering holes. The Button Ball Tavern was one of those places that seemed to have been in existence forever. It originally opened in the 1930s and was licensed as a tavern, which meant only beer, wine and hard cider were allowed to be sold. Hard liquor was not permitted.[45]

In 1951, John Kostan, then operator of the Button Ball, was arrested after two inspectors from the state liquor control commission and a Fairfield policeman found several bottles of liquor in a container outside the tavern. Kostan was found guilty of keeping liquor on the premises and was fined $100.[46]

"I believe it was 1975 when I bought the Button Ball Tavern," said Fred Fugazzi. At the time, he and his then-wife lived in a three-family house. "My neighbor John Maleck found out we were house hunting, approached me and suggested that I consider buying his bar as opposed to a house," said Fugazzi. "He worked construction and only worked the bar a couple times a week. His mother, Kay, was the permittee and ran the place during the day, and his brother Stan took care of the place at night. I looked into the business and found that they were turning a small profit. I saw the potential to increase business and decided to buy it."

The Button Ball was located in a small strip mall on Black Rock Turnpike, next to Scott's Stationery, a popular convenience store. "The inside was rectangular and smaller in comparison than most bars," said Fugazzi. "When you entered, the bar was on the right and extended about three-quarters of the way to the rear. There was room for about a dozen bar stools. Directly across from the bar there were three old-fashioned booths. I later replaced the booths with four tables and chairs. Beyond the bar was a pool table, juke box and pin ball machine. At the end there were rest rooms and the kitchen."

The Button Ball was a neighborhood bar and the clientele was mostly blue collar. "There were a lot of people from the building trades, carpenters, plumbers, electricians and equipment operators," said Fugazzi. "Regulars from other occupations included artists, teachers from both Fairfield University and NYU, antiques dealers, sales people, policemen, firemen and many others. The conversation was always interesting and often lively."

Eventually, the Button Ball started offering food in addition to beer and wine.

"Shortly after taking ownership, I increased the daily menu to include hamburgers, hot dogs, kielbasa, fish cakes and a variety of sandwiches," said Fugazzi. "We had a different lunch special each day that came with potatoes and vegetables: stuffed peppers, meatloaf, mac and cheese, stuffed cabbage, shepherd's pie and roast beef. With the daily lunch specials, our weekday business picked up considerably. The Saturday daytime business was not up to expectations, so I offered hot dogs boiled in beer with the works for five cents."

The hot dog special worked and it drew the crowds in. "I discontinued that special and offered hot roast beef sandwiches for twenty-five cents," said Fugazzi.

One of the main draws of the Button Ball was its pool table. Fugazzi said:

To keep everyone interested and involved, I put together a pool team and entered them in the Park City Pool League. One of my female customers put together a women's team and started their own league. I was going to sponsor a softball team and the response was so great I ended up sponsoring two teams. I also sponsored a bowling team. It took almost a year, but the place finally became what I had in mind from the beginning. It was like a miniature Cheers. Even though I was able to increase business and bring in new customers, everyone got to know each other and it was a friendly place where people enjoyed themselves.

The Button Ball was loved by many, but sadly, it wasn't meant to last. Fred Fugazzi eventually sold the business to Ron Tierney and his mother. They, in turn, sold it to Fred Figlar. In 1991, Tony DeLibero reopened the bar as Tony D's Café, and in 2002, the building was demolished to make room for a large CVS pharmacy.[47]

3

TEA HOUSES

All of the Cheer, None of the Inebriation

While men had taverns as places to socialize and enjoy food and drink, it wasn't until the 1800s when women focused on setting up public spaces of their own. Enter the tearoom, a more refined and genteel setting where ladies could meet and socialize while enjoying a snack or small meal.

"Women, particularly those New Englanders who could trace their ancestry to Colonial times, became supporters of the preservation of American antiquities," wrote Jan Whitaker on her blog "Vintage Tea Rooms."[48] "Newly possible car travel encouraged them to explore former taverns in the countryside. Next they began to open tea rooms that celebrated Early America, many with names and signs from tavern days. It was as though taverns had returned, clean, ultra-respectable and without liquor and drunkenness. Tea, after all, was known as 'the cup that cheers but does not inebriate.'"

The town green was home to one such establishment, frequented by visitors who came to spend summers at the beach. The Old Academy Tea Room offered afternoon tea, but before that, the building served as a school. The academy was organized in 1802, chartered in 1804 and operated until 1887. It was revived briefly as a residential school for New York boys and then a public library building.[49] Eventually, though, the building sat unused and neglected, and nature began to take over; trees grew up around it, and squirrels and mice made it their home. It was then that "the Misses Porter" from Philadelphia came to its rescue.

The sisters, Susan and Emily, had the idea of creating a tearoom in Fairfield. They enjoyed their summers in Fairfield and wanted to create a business that would enable them to keep visiting every year. With barely any financial backing, the women went in search of a building that was of little use to anyone else.[50]

Despite advice from outsiders that the academy was beyond repair, the sisters had a vision. Yes, the building had been neglected. Inside, vestiges from its days as a schoolhouse remained. Old desks, chairs, books and papers filled the rooms, while the walls and blackboards crumbled to the floors. The women were undaunted; they removed the furnace, painted over the blackboards and repaired the plaster and the woodwork. The walls were painted a soft yellow and the floor was painted gray. Tables were covered with linen and an old school bench sat in one corner, welcoming visitors to sign the guest book.[51]

It was said that the women's motto was, "The best of everything at a moderate cost." Since they were strapped for cash, they often were only able to buy one pound of sugar and a small bag of flour at a time.[52] Yet somehow they made it work.

In a newspaper clipping from June 16, 1915, an article details the opening of the tearoom.[53] Mrs. Henry S. Glover invited guests to the establishment the day before the formal opening. The article described the scene:

> *Some of the chairs and old trays used at the tea rooms are from* [the Hobart and Porter] *houses. Round rag rugs dot the floor near high-back rockers. A warming pan leans near the ancient fireplace. The little black tables are simple, quaint pieces of furniture and an old academy bench, painted black, bears the initials of children who have long ago grown up and passed away.*

The description of the tearoom's opening day is charming. "The decorations were kept as nearly as possible to wild flowers and to old-fashioned shrubs, which were placed in simple jars and pots, quite in harmony with the colonial note."[54]

The times may have been progressive enough that two single women were able to own their own business, but there was still plenty of room for growth in the equality department. An "ancient colored retainer" was quoted in the 1915 newspaper article, dispelling a myth that the academy was haunted. "Oh, sho!" the article read. "Dey's jus' rats, and sometimes dey soun' jes' lak sho enough humans."[55] Fairfield still had a way to go.

The Old Academy Tea Room was a popular gathering spot for the women of the town, and events were often held there. An article from 1915 noted that Angeline S. Donley gave a talk titled "Fashion in Furnishing."[56]

As the seasons passed, the Porter sisters were able to improve the building and add to their supplies. In a written history owned by the Fairfield Museum, the author writes:

I visited the Tea Room yesterday and looked back upon the changes and growth…The gift shop has entirely outgrown the first floor and fills the second where the girls camped out those first summers. The business has grown from tea to lunches and from lunches to dinners and outside catering.

At the time, there was one cook and two waitresses who helped ice the cakes and make salads and sandwiches. "One day we sent out 500 small cakes and ten layer cakes besides our regular inside orders and another day we served lunch and tea to about eighty people, had a dinner of thirty and catered for a tea and evening dance." Even today this would be a huge undertaking. One has to wonder how they managed without the use of a KitchenAid mixer or an industrial-sized oven.

The author concluded with her own review:

Fresh wild flowers will greet you at every turn. The soft mauve Joe-pie-weed in a vase of the same tone against the clear yellow walls or black-eyed-susans blending walls and furniture together, purple iron weed or yellow golden rod according to the season. Long rush brooms stand by the open fires and bright colored calico covered pillows adorn the old school benches. It is just the place for a rainy day as one is sure to meet a friend and only the Tea Room with its delicious cakes and iced drinks can satisfy the youthful appetites. Till late in the Autumn, when after a long walk one welcomes a cup of hot tea before a crackling fire, the hospitable doors are open and it is with real regret that we say "good bye" at the end of the season to friends and Tea Room alike.[57]

There are other reviews on record, as well. In a society column called "Topics of the Town," writer Carolyn Morgan asked, "Where else can one get such delicious, thin-as-wafer sandwiches, such melt-in-your-mouth cakes, chocolate and spice, or such delicious iced chocolate?"[58]

In an undated magazine clipping preserved in the Fairfield Museum and History Center's scrapbook, an unidentified author wrote, "In a little scoot through New England we ran across at Fairfield, Conn., 'The old Academy Tea Room.' Please note that they did not call it 'Ye olde'—though as a matter of fact, the building is very old indeed. It is conducted by two young Philadelphia women, the daughters of a former Philadelphia physician.

Here we had real food. Delightful coffee and home-made ice cream up to the best Philadelphia standard."[59]

In 1925, Mrs. Samuel H. Wheeler entertained about fifty guests in honor of her daughter who was leaving for Europe. After the event, the Porter sisters closed the tearoom for the season. Susan and her brother William left for Philadelphia, and Emily went to Bristol, Rhode Island, for a few days before returning to Philadelphia.[60] The Old Academy Tea Room continued to open each summer for many years after.

Quaint Little Cottage by the Shore

The Old Academy wasn't the only tea house in town. Ladies could also find their repast at the Ebenezer Silliman House, which was located at 418 Jennings Road. It operated as a tea house until the 1930s. In 1966, the house was moved to 405 North Cedar Road to avoid demolition.[61]

Southport was also in on the tea scene. In 1810, Eleazer Bulkley built a house at 935 Harbor Road. One hundred years later, a group of women gathered to start a fund for a visiting nurse in the village. In the summer of 1913, they opened the Set-a-Spell Tea House as a way to raise money for their venture. A flier from the time described the tea house as "the Quaint Little Cottage By the Shore." It was only open on Fridays. One would imagine it must have been the place to be for all the ladies in Southport. There, by the water, they played bridge and snacked on ice cream, tea, sandwiches, cake and coffee. There was also a gift shop.

The first two years, profits from the Set-a-Spell weren't enough to employ a nurse on a permanent basis, but enough money was raised to "relieve many different cases of want and sickness." In February of that year, Mrs. James Brown was hired to act as a visiting nurse and social worker. Within four months, she had visited ninety-five different homes and "called many times where she found need and sickness."[62]

The Set-a-Spell's location, on a coveted parcel of waterside property, seems as if it must have been quiet and serene. However, the sweet, respectable tea house wasn't safe from hooligans, even in the early twentieth century. A newspaper article entitled "Slouch Hatted Culprits Busy in Fairfield" stated that a "hold-up occurred in front of the Set-a-Spell tea house when Miss Mary Lee of Harbor Road was accosted. Her screams frightened the robbers away. The Misses Anna and Katherine Russell of

Open only on Fridays, the Set-a-Spell teahouse in Southport was a place where ladies could gather for sandwiches, ice cream and tea. *Courtesy of the Fairfield Museum and History Center.*

Willow street, sisters of William Russell, postmaster, were stopped near the same place. Some jewelry was taken from them."[63] The incident must have been the talk of the tea house for weeks after. The Set-a-Spell operated until 1950, when the building was demolished.

Up on the Hill

Over in the Greenfield Hill section of town, ladies gathered at the Tea Time Tavern. Opening day was on June 12, 1912. The tea house was a project of the Thimble Club (the predecessor of the Junior League of Bridgeport). The women made layettes for the Visiting Nurse Association, the Red Cross, Bridgeport Hospital, the Welfare Department and the Main Street Day Nursery. They started the tea house at the summer residence of Dr. and Mrs. DeVer H. Warner (of the Warner corset manufacturing business) as a way to make money for material and supplies.[64]

Thursdays during the summer months were "tea days," and a sign in the shape of a cup and saucer would be hung out in front of the house on Hillside Road. A report from 1913 noted, "Out on the lawn under the spruce trees where the shade is dense and cool, tables are placed for bridge. They are far enough away from the tea tables to be undisturbed by the small talk over the tea cups."[65]

Indeed, the setting sounded like a lovely place for women to gather. In a newsletter, the Tea Time Tavern was described:

> *The building is well equipped for the serving of lunches and for entertaining visitors. Everything is dainty and attractive and the porches, which command a beautiful view, are furnished with rattan chairs, porch swings, etc. while on each of the tables was a centerpiece of flowers. From the porches a beautiful view of the surrounding country is to be had.[66]*

A committee of workers were appointed for each week, and sandwiches were made on the porch. Said the newsletter, "The menu is inviting. One may have hot or iced tea and coffee or fruit punch, a choice of sandwiches of three varieties and very delicious cake." One of the volunteers, Miss Hurlburt, baked all of the cakes. She became so well-known as a baker that she gave up her teaching job and went into the baking business. A menu showed that tea, coffee and lemonade were fifteen cents; sandwiches ("Tea Time," lettuce or chicken) were fifteen cents; and cake (fudge, chocolate marshmallow or layer) were ten cents. A bridge table for the afternoon was one dollar.[67]

An article from 1915 detailed an event given by members of the Visiting Nurse Association. For a one-dollar admission, ladies received "conveyance from Library Corner" for the trip, which was approximately two miles each way.[68]

"The Tea Time Tavern is ideally set among a group of tall hemlock and from its southern side may be obtained a wonderful view of miles of countryland and Long Island Sound," the article reported.

The women played bridge, and local girls gave a dance recital. Ice cream, tea and cake were served. "The rooms of the Tavern itself were attractively decorated with bouquets of garden flowers. A three-piece orchestra furnished the music for dancing at both sessions of the fete."[69] One of the main events of the day was the opportunity for guests to have their pictures taken. A photographer was employed to take tintypes of the guests.

The Tea Time Tavern continued to operate through the summer of 1917. Some years later, the Greenfield Hill Village Improvement Society put together *A Book for the Cook: Old Fashioned Receipts for New Fashioned Kitchens.* Perhaps some of those recipes were handed down from members of the Thimble Society, such as these for short cake and angel cake.[70]

SHORT CAKE

A piece of lard the size of an egg, the same quantity of butter, a large cupful of flour, rub all well together with a little ice cold water and a small quantity of salt. When well mixed and shaped like a ball, roll it out well, double it and roll again three times, then roll out thin, cut the size and shape desired and bake.

ANGEL CAKE

Whites of 11 eggs well beaten, 1½ cups of sugar, little salt, take 1 cup of flour and 1 teaspoon of cream of tartar, sift together four times through a sieve; 1 teaspoon vanilla, bake from 40 to 60 minutes in a deep round pan not greased; let it cool before taking from the pan upside down.

During the time of temperance, tearooms provided women with places to socialize and enjoy light meals. Their popularity waned as the 1950s approached, however, and larger cafés and luncheonettes began to take over.

SOUTHPORT'S GRAND RESTAURANTS

M ost people today recognize the Tide Mill building on Harbor Road as the place where they went to the doctor. In 1958, Dr. William Kueffner moved his pediatric offices from the corner of Reef and Post Roads to the architecturally-unique building on the bridge connecting the Sasco Hill area to Southport. Here, the town children went for their yearly check-ups and emergency stitches. They played with the typewriter and the antique cash register in the waiting room and looked out the windows to watch the boats on the river. Meanwhile, teenagers rode their bikes to the mill to go fishing and crabbing and to just hang out. "In the early 1970s, someone spray painted 'Legalize Pot' on the low wall along the upper-right part of the road," reminisced Beth Bilyard. "Later, someone added the suffix 'atoes.' It was there for years."[71] The Tide Mill building was a historic, iconic structure that every Fairfielder knew about. But what many don't realize is that long before the building was a doctor's office, it had several incarnations—including more than a few as a restaurant.

It's believed that the original mill was built in 1724 by Joseph Perry and was operated by his son, Micah, and Micah's son, Jabez. In 1779, the British landed in Fairfield and burned down the mill (along with much of the town). It was built again, only to burn down two more times, once in 1802 and again in 1855.[72] The mill, apparently, was to have more lives than a cat.

An article in the *Southport Packet* from October 1987 explored these different uses of the mill. At the time, author Christopher B. Nevins,

SPINNING WHEEL – Southport, Connecticut – Tel. 9-4822

Once a working mill, the Spinning Wheel restaurant was popular for people arriving both by car and boat. *Courtesy of the author.*

then curator of the Fairfield Historical Society, wrote of Regina Kiley, one of the last remaining people to remember the mill when it was in operation. In the late 1800s, the mill was used to produce "the finest rye flour and the best bolted corn meal for pudding and milk." By that time, though, Fairfield's agricultural days were coming to an end, and the mill eventually ceased operations.[73] This, however, was just the beginning for the mill's future use as a restaurant.

Clarence B. Sturges purchased the building and remodeled it in a Tudor style, complete with lead windows, white walls and half timbers. In 1924, Tide Mill Tavern opened under the management of Margaret S. Taylor.[74] It was a beautiful building with an even better view. "The restaurant appealed to the growing suburban population of the Fairfield area, a pleasant place to stop on a drive along the shore. There was even a dock for passing pleasure craft, and overnight guests could be accommodated in the upstairs chambers," wrote Nevins.

"The restaurant was extremely popular with local residents as a place to dine in a comfortable, friendly environment," wrote John Payne in the October 1996 edition of the *Southport Packet*. "There were virtually no family restaurants in Southport and very few in Fairfield from the mid-twenties through the period of World War II."

Capturing the spirit of the times, Fairfield resident Henry Miller created this pen-and-ink restaurant scene in 1928. *Courtesy of Joan Woods.*

During the warm weather, guests would sail their boats up the Mill River and stop for lunch or dinner at the restaurant. On the second floor of the building, several guest rooms had been added for those wishing to spend the night."[75]

As one of the few restaurants in town at the time, it was a popular place for dinner parties, bridge luncheons and bridal showers.

"The Tide Mill Tavern continued to operate successfully, though modestly, through the 1930s and into the 1940s and it was able to do so without having a liquor license," wrote Payne.

The menu from the time implored visitors to visit the gift shop:

Look at the costume jewelry; many pieces suggest the enchanting jewels worn by your great grandmother of long ago. Here and there you will find authentic reproductions of English silver on copper—a tea caddy, a fluted Bon Bon—lovely wedding gifts. The Audubon Bird Plates are finished examples of workmanship. The reproduction of early American Pressed Glass you will see in constant use on our dining room tables. Our flower containers and arrangements have an interest all their own. The variety of cards fill every need. While you are looking for just the right one, the young members of your party will find amusement in the toy corner.

Despite its popularity, the restaurant struggled, presumably because of the lack of a liquor license. Permits were applied for but routinely denied. Payne wrote:

Dinner guests sometimes had a cocktail or two at home before going to the Tavern. Most folks, though, went without a pre-dinner drink. When former resident Norman Morse was a young man, he and his family lived on Sasco Hill and often dined at the Tide Mill Tavern….Norman would occasionally collect a few friends in the early evening, prepare cocktails and hors d'oeuvres and sail his 20½ foot gaff-headed sloop Diana *up the Mill River to anchor outside the casement windows of the eating porch of the Tide Mill Tavern. He and his friends would "open the bar" and enjoy their drinks on the boat while toasting the people inside "who were perfectly dry," eating their meals, without alcoholic beverage, only a few feet away.*

Over the years, the tavern continued under various managers until 1942, when it was purchased by Elaine D. Tottle and her son, William.[76] The pair were the proprietors of the Spinning Wheel Inn at Redding Ridge, a restaurant some thirteen miles away in what still is a very rural section of Fairfield County. The Redding location was very successful, but during World War II, it closed for four years due to gasoline rationing. It was during this time that Tottle owned the Spinning Wheel Mill in Southport. According to local legend, Tottle would drive from Redding to Southport each morning, picking up staff members along the way.[77]

In 1946, the Redding location reopened, but two years later, there was a fire, which forced Tottle to again close the restaurant for a time. Undaunted, she rebuilt the structure, and three years later, she opened yet another Spinning Wheel, this time in Sarasota, Florida. The restaurants then became seasonal, with the Redding location opening the first Saturday in May and closing the Sunday after Thanksgiving and the Florida location opening on New Year's Eve and closing right after Easter.[78]

A menu from the Spinning Wheel Mill shows a variety of options for dinner. Choices for the first course included a fruit juice frappé, a tomato juice cocktail, a soup of the day, clam chowder, vichyssoise, shrimp cocktail and jellied madrilene (a consommé with tomato) with sour cream. Main courses ran the gamut of seafood, beef and chicken. Options included Southport Stuffed Clams (the description read, "An old sailors receipt"), creamed chicken and mushrooms, southern-glazed sugar-cured ham, Cape Cod scallops, Famous Old Williamsburg Chicken Pot Pie, charcoal-broiled lamb chops and lobster served one of four ways: browned in fresh butter and sherry, Newburg (simmered in sherry and cream and thickened with eggs), thermidore (combined with mushrooms and rich sauce) and Cardinal (heavy cream and hollandaise, topped with Parmesan cheese). Dinners were served with a relish bowl, vegetables, choice of potatoes, assorted breads, dessert and a beverage. "Little Folks" (those twelve and under) were given the option of soup or tomato juice, creamed chicken or broiled chopped steak, vegetables, milk, bread and dessert. Nary a chicken nugget or hot dog was to be found.

A flier for the Spinning Wheel said, "There is a warmth of hospitality to greet the guests and an unsurpassed view of Southport Harbor with the blue waters of the Sound off shore and in the distance, when the weather is fine, the outline of Long Island can be clearly seen."

Payne, who himself frequented the restaurant in the 1940s, recalled, "The food at the Inn was excellent, traditional New England–style cooking. It was highlighted by homemade soups, fresh-baked rolls and sticky buns. When in season, delicious local vegetables were served. Meals would be topped off with memorable homemade desserts."[79]

At the bottom of the menu, diners were forewarned that "fifteen minutes are required to cook your food properly."

An article from an issue of the *Redding Times* looked at the success of Elaine Tottle's restaurant empire. "Elaine Tottle is a Gore of Baltimore and brought with her to Redding in 1925 not only her best southern recipes and three colored servants, but the kind of entertaining that has almost vanished from this scientific, mercenary age." (Interestingly, in the article, the author gives a nod to not only Tottle but also the "youngest, good looking waitress." Oh my.)[80]

When Tottle decided it was time to close the Southport location, she sold it to the Galaske family, who bought it for $33,500. In 1954, Caroline Lipscomb expressed her interest in purchasing the building. She submitted an application for a zoning waver to permit the restaurant to be converted into an apartment house. Many of the neighbors supported the request on the grounds that an apartment house would bring less traffic to the area than the restaurant did.[81] Throughout the years, the inn operated under the names of the Mill River Inn, the Tide Mill Inn and the Tide Mill Tavern until 1960, when it was converted into offices.

Elaine Tottle wrote a cookbook called *Whispers from the Spinning Wheel Kitchen*. The limited-run paperback included her favorite recipes, as well as a short story of her own crafting. Following are recipes from the book.[82]

CHICKEN DELICIOUS
[This recipe is still served on occasion at the current
Spinning Wheel Inn in Redding.]

2 cups chicken stock
4 tablespoons butter
4 tablespoons flour
½ teaspoon salt
Mace and cayenne pepper, to taste
1½ cups cooked chicken, cubed
1 cup mushrooms, sautéed
Bread crumbs
1 egg, beaten
Strips of bacon

Scald chicken stock. Melt butter, then add flour and stir to a roux. Pour scalding chicken stock on roux gradually, beating smooth. Add seasonings. Combine this mixture with chicken and mushrooms. Chill. Form into rolls 3½ by 2 inches and roll in coarse bread crumbs. Dip in egg and again in bread crumbs, then wrap with a strip of bacon. Oven-brown and serve.

KOSSUTH CAKE

2 eggs, separated
½ cup water
1 cup sugar
1 cup flour
1 teaspoon baking powder
¼ teaspoon salt
½ teaspoon vanilla

Beat egg yolks until thick, add water, sugar, flour sifted with baking powder and salt. Fold in whipped egg whites, add vanilla. Bake 30 minutes in layer cake pan in oven 350 degrees F. When cake has cooled, split, fill with one pint of cream whipped, sweetened with 2 tablespoons powdered sugar and flavored with one teaspoon vanilla. Ice top with following Chocolate Glaze, cut cake in pie shaped pieces and serve.

CHOCOLATE GLAZE

¾ cup powdered sugar
½ cup melted chocolate
1 egg
½ teaspoon vanilla

Mix all together until smooth. Heat over boiling water until thin enough to
pour over cake.

SPINNING WHEEL ONION SOUP

12 medium onions
4 tablespoons butter
2 tablespoons brown sugar
2 quarts hot soup stock
Salt
Black pepper
Rounds of toast
Grated American cheese
Paprika

Peel onions, quarter and slice thin. Melt butter in frying pan, add onions
and fry very brown. Stir in brown sugar, cook 3 minutes and add to hot
stock. Season with salt and black pepper.

Sprinkle rounds of toast thickly with grated cheese, dust with paprika,
brown in oven. Serve the soup very hot and float the toast rounds on top.

Grated Parmesan cheese may also be passed if you like extra cheese.

THE PEQUOT INN

The restaurant at the old mill wasn't the only game in town, however. In
1922, two years before the Tide Mill Tavern opened under Margaret S.
Taylor's watch, a grand Victorian home in Southport was converted into
an inn.[83] The house originally belonged to Oliver Bulkley, a retired shipping
merchant, and was passed down to his daughters, Annie and Katie. In 1920,
they sold it to Charles Keats, who transformed it into the Pequot Inn. In
1945, Everett and Dorothy Whiting bought the inn and then eventually

leased it to Arthur Hawes of Worcester, Massachusetts, and his assistant Barbara Locke. An advertisement from the *Fairfield News* on March 29 noted that the Pequot Inn was reopening on Sunday, March 31, 1946. "After extensive redecorating, we are again prepared to serve you the finest in foods under the supervision of Edmund Waide, one of New England's foremost chefs," the ad read.

In 1952, Lucia J. Parks wrote an article about the inn for the *New Southport Chronicle*. In it, she described the setting:

> *The two dining-rooms (once a sitting room and music room) are gay in a paper of scarlet with a brilliant pattern of white morning glories climbing a bamboo trellis. White tables and chairs and snowy white linen carry out the tone set by gleaming white mantels in each room. The south dining room, particularly, is enchanting, with its large medallion over the mirror and its stained glass birds and fruits, flowers and butterflies about the bay windows.*

Parks notes that there was also a gift shop where visitors could buy things such as silverware, pottery, jams, jellies and spices.

Those coming to dine at the Pequot Inn were treated to a fine meal. It might begin with a glass of tomato juice, followed by corn on the cob, a garden salad with French dressing and hot rolls. Decadent lobster Newburg, topped with a rich cream sauce, was served and, for dessert, a macaroon cake with ice cream and chocolate sauce. The price range for dinner was $2.75 to $3.50.[84]

THE CENTER OF ATTENTION

In 1925, Tony Tambakis and Peter Caloyianis opened a restaurant on the Post Road in Fairfield aptly named Center Restaurant.[85] Everyone knew "the Center." Located next to a beauty parlor and a bakery, the restaurant was ideally situated to become a prominent eatery in town. In 1927, the pair added Elias Papageorge to the partnership. The Connecticut Turnpike wouldn't be built for another thirty-one years, so the Post Road was the main thoroughfare for traffic from neighboring towns. People passing through would stop at the Center for breakfast, lunch and dinner. In 1934, Papageorge left the Center Restaurant to start his own eatery, the Club Grill in Westport. In 1958, Papageorge's sons, George and Angelus, bought the Center when they returned from World War II. "George—he was one hard-working son of a gun," said his son, Tom Papageorge.[86] He explained how, when his father was in high school, he would take the trolley from Fairfield to Westport early in the morning to go to the Club Grill. There he would serve breakfast, get back on the trolley and go to high school. In the afternoons, he would go to football practice and then take the trolley back to Westport to serve dinner.

Tom remembers being put to work in the restaurant from the time he was just a young child. "I was probably six or seven," said Papageorge. "If they needed a dishwasher, I'd get drafted for a few hours. I just remember the sinks being so high."

The restaurant served American diner–style food and had a bar. "There were two lamps on each side of the front door," said Papageorge. "The room

The Center Restaurant opened in the heart of Fairfield in 1925 and was open for nearly six decades. *Courtesy of the Fairfield Museum and History Center.*

to the left had booths and the counter. The dining room on the right became the bar in the 1930s." At one point, an Art Deco–style partition was put in and the bar got flipped to the other side.

"They were working off a low profit margin with the food," said Papageorge. "They recognized they were making more money off drinks." In those days, it was all about hard liquor. "They'd make the drinks from scratch," said Papageorge. A whiskey sour would be made with fresh lemons and a simple syrup made from two parts sugar to one part water. "You'd boil the crap out of it and make it thick," said Papageorge. "They were drinking these awful things," he said. "Old-fashioneds with simple syrup, bitters and rye, Port wine before dinner, cream sherry after dinner. People got slogged." In the 1950s, he said, men would come in at lunchtime and have a shot and a beer and then go back to work. In the 1960s, he said, there was "a lot of booze at lunchtime." Men would have two or three martinis, Manhattans or Rob Roys, at lunch. "This was a time when the cops were more people-friendly," said Papageorge. "They saw you crapped out, they'd give you a ride home." Papageorge credits that "friendliness" as a result of World War II. "There was a common goal, to defeat Hitler," he said. "There was that connection to community. Everybody knew everybody."

For nearly six decades, the Center Restaurant was the place to go for dinner and drinks. *Courtesy of the Fairfield Museum and History Center.*

A newspaper article from September 1959 noted the restaurant's thirty-fourth anniversary and recent renovations.[87] The "gas light era" was revived at the restaurant with the installation of gas coach lamps on each side of the entrance, making it the first instance in Fairfield of a return to gas for outdoor lighting. The gas lamps outside the front door were lit, and they offered nickel hot dogs and beers. "It drew huge crowds," said Papageorge. "It was like a circus."

In 1962, the restaurant celebrated a "1920 menu with 1920 prices" for two days. The menu included a five-cent cup of coffee, a twenty-five-cent cocktail and a seventy-five-cent dinner. In a newspaper article at the time, the Papageorge brothers were quoted as saying, "The good old days are gone forever, except for two days each year at our restaurant."[88]

When the 1970s hit, things began to change. "In the '70s and '80s, everyone talked about networking, but they had already had it down," said Papageorge. He watched as the trends began to shift. "It was a big transition," he said. "People started drinking white wine and flavored brandies of lower proof. [The liquor companies] were targeting women," he said.

Another change at the time was the broadcasting of NFL games. Tom Papageorge saw an opportunity there. "I thought, we should get a TV and hook up an antenna to draw a crowd," he said. The plan worked. The football games drew huge crowds. The Center did start to face competition in the summertime with the bars located on the beach. Surfside and Beachside offered live music, which drew the younger crowds. "I said, 'Let's see if we can get them off the beach,'" said Papageorge. He experimented with getting different bands to play at the Center. "We tried to mix it up so we weren't so dependent on one act," he said. He developed relationships with musicians from the nearby University of Bridgeport, and he also hired a horn band from Andrew Warde High School called Threshold. "They were a pack of geniuses," said Papageorge.

Maureen Delaney remembers going to the Center on many occasions. "It was mainly middle class families," she said.[89] "The Center Restaurant was the place we congregated on Friday nights. The front section of the restaurant faced the Post Road and the corner entrance was to the bar area. Women sat at the tables and our significant others would get our drinks. The band was at the very end. It was a small venue but we all went on Friday or Saturday nights because of the bands. I drank whiskey sours and my husband drank beer from the tap. Harvey Wallbangers were popular because I had one once…and never again," she said.

When the drinking age changed in 1972, Papageorge was faced with new challenges. "The law changed from twenty-one to eighteen and it was like the Oklahoma Gold Rush," he said. "I had to familiarize myself with different school yearbooks, because there weren't photo IDs back then. The place was full of high school kids. How much fun can that be?" he said. Eventually, however, the younger patrons shifted toward the Nautilus because of its close proximity to the beach.

After nearly six decades in business, the Center Restaurant had run its course. Papageorge sold the business in 1976. Its ideal location, however, meant that the building wouldn't stand empty for very long.

6

ALL THAT JAZZ

Mr. Music Brings Big Names to the Continental

In 1954, Fairfield was about to have its socks knocked off. At the junction of Villa Avenue and King's Highway, on the site of a former restaurant called Al's Cozy Corner and then the Donald Duck, the Continental—a restaurant-cum-jazz club—was born.

William Ratzenberger, aka "Mr. Music," traveled throughout the United States in the 1930s and '40s playing with famous bands led by people such as Artie Shaw, Lee Miles, Eddie Rogers, Anthony Trini and many others.[90] He began playing trumpet with the William Malone Orchestra at the Ritz Ballroom in New York City. His musical career was interrupted, however, when he was called to serve in World War II. Yet he still kept up with his music. He was a sergeant in charge of the U.S. Army Band at Fort H.G. Wright, Fisher's Island, New London. In 1945, he returned home and opened the Music Center on Fairfield Avenue, which had practice rooms, a rehearsal hall and a recording studio. There, Ratzenberger taught the trombone and the trumpet. In 1954, he and his wife, Millie, opened the Continental restaurant, which specialized in Hungarian cuisine and featured music on the weekends. The building, situated on a triangle-shaped piece of land, had a curving façade, which was said to look like a grand piano.

"We used to go all the time when I was little," said Susan Burke.[91] "I remember they had a painting on the wall and the lights in the buildings' windows were painted in yellow black-light paint to make them glow. I was fascinated by it when I was a kid." The mural was painted by local artist Leslie Fairchild. The décor was luxurious. The floors were plush red velvet, and white cherubim would look upon diners from the corners of the ceilings. "The bar was to the right and it was circular," said Jerry Buswell, who played drums at the Continental.[92] "When you entered the dining room it was like an old time 1940s night club with red table cloths and white napkins on tables for four. The one-step stage was in the back of the room where the Ed Graf trio would play or whoever was the highlight of the Friday night." During the week, the Continental Trio—Julius Ehrenwerth on cello, Gizella Ehrenwerth on violin and James Leon on piano—would perform.[93] On Friday nights, top-line guest musicians would entertain the crowds. "I was lucky enough to play drums with Ella Fitzgerald, Teddy Wilson, Maxine Sullivan, and Maynard Ferguson at the Continental," said Buswell. "Usually people would eat before 9:00 p.m. and then the music would start and cocktails all night," he said.

Joann Dos Santos remembered the Continental fondly. "They had the best jazz. Many of the best jazz greats came up to play there, such as Clark Terry, Teddy Wilson, Zoot Sims, Kenny Burrell…the list goes on and on. The house band was good as well. Bill had a reel-to-reel tape recorder and recorded every session."[94]

Bob Delancy felt at home at the Continental and considered the Ratzenbergers family. "My mom worked at the Continental as a hostess/cashier so I had two mothers: Millie and Marie," he said. When Delancy was twenty-two years old, he started working at the Continental as well. "Millie molded me to her way as a young waiter. Eventually we thought alike and we got along beautifully. The greatest experience at the Continental was for a young person to work with and learn from the finest of people. The customers were VIPs and were like family. Lots of power, privilege and prestige came into that restaurant."[95]

Reviewer Patty Malkin described a night out at the Continental in her "Dining Out" column in a 1972 edition of the *Connecticut Sunday Herald*. "Mrs. Ratzenberger (Bill and Mrs. Ratzenberger have owned the restaurant for 19 years) recommended that we…try the Cannelloni Piemontese…It cost only $1 and makes a marvelous appetizer." Malkin points out that "Chef Leonardo Riccio is responsible for the delicious fare…All this takes place in an intimate atmosphere with a certain old-world charm. Much of the warmth comes from the presence of Mr. and Mrs. Ratzenberger who enjoy the happenings at their establishment every bit as much as the patrons."[96]

Malkin then went on to rave about the veal scallopine bolognese and the chicken valdostana. "After dinner," she wrote, "we simply were not ready to bid farewell…so we lingered over Stingers and chatted with owner Bill Ratzenberger."

Millie Ratzenberger was the hostess with the mostest at the Continental. Here she is seen welcoming two guests to the restaurant. *Courtesy of Bob Delancy.*

Howard Meyer worked at the Continental as a bartender and said that hard-liquor cocktails were all the rage. "People would order Southern Comfort Manhattans, Rusty Nails, Stingers," he said.[97]

Harkening back to the days when diners would enjoy a stiff after-dinner drink, the Stinger is a mix of crème de menthe and brandy, shaken and served in a cocktail glass. The origins of this drink are unclear, but a recipe for it appears in Tom Bullock's *Ideal Bartender*, published in 1917.

STINGER—COUNTRY CLUB STYLE
Use a large Mixing glass; fill with Lump Ice.
1 jigger Old Brandy.
1 pony white Creme de Menthe.
Shake well; strain into Cocktail glass and serve.

Advertisements in the local paper offered a special menu on Mondays, Tuesdays and Thursdays, from 5:00 to 8:00 p.m. For $5.95, diners could get their choice of beef paprikas, stuffed peppers, chicken paprikas, beef goulash or stuffed cabbage, served with soup or juice, salad, a beverage and homemade Hungarian pastry. Cocktails were $1.00.

In her "Dining Out" column in the *Sunday Herald* from 1963, Barbara Graham wrote, "Recently redecorated, the main dining room now features striking Renaissance décor. Specialties: Lobster Fra Diavolo, veal scallopine Florentine, chicken Marengo, which shares the honors with a long list of broiler, seafood and continental favorites."[98]

Graham continued in her signature flowery style:

> *If there were such an instrument as a gustatometer, operating in Geiger-counter style, the distinctively styled Continental Restaurant would give it quite a buzz for directly inside the neat white façade is the palate-happy hideout of a host of diners-out to whom Bill and Millie Ratzenberger are both "pied piper and shepherd." Though never have I donned a dolman or clanked a saber (horses don't seem to understand me), I do get along splendidly with the tenderloin of Beef Brochette bedded in rice, glad that they're chunks of beef transfixed instead of me, and these toothsome nuggets as prepared at the Continental are particularly noble to the tusk.*

One has to wonder if she wrote the review after a few Stingers.

She concludes, "But the lures of this spot are not by any means confined to the menu. Ever since the restaurant opened in 1954, it has reflected the philosophy of owner Bill Ratzenberger which places equal emphasis on attractive surroundings, good service and 'music for listening' as the fitting accompaniments for good dining."

In 1979, the Ratzenbergers retired from the restaurant business. Bill devoted his time to Jet-Tone, his business manufacturing world-renowned musical instrument mouthpieces. He passed away on October 5, 1983. A memorial concert of jazz was held a month later at Ottavio's restaurant.[99] Millie passed away in May 2008.[100]

OPEN TWENTY-FOUR HOURS

The Diners of Fairfield

Fine dining is all well and good, but nothing says comfort like a good diner. With countless menu choices, breakfast served twenty-four hours a day and ethnic specialties, diners are the restaurants of the masses.

A photograph in the Sunday, January 2, 1955 edition of the *Sunday Post* honors the first restaurant license that was distributed in Fairfield. Dr. Richard E. Caron, director of the Fairfield Health Department, presented co-owners James Slingo and Charles Heim with a certificate for the Fairfielder Diner, which was located at 925 Post Road.[101] Hamburgers were twenty cents; twenty-five cents if you wanted tomato with it. Specials changed daily but would feature things like soft shell crab on toast, fish cakes and beans, calves' liver and bacon and grilled ham steak with potato and vegetable. To the locals, the Fairfielder was known as "Jimmy's," after the owner.

The Fairfielder may have been the first restaurant to have an official license, however, there were other diners serving up breakfast and sandwiches long before that. Even today, residents get confused between the Fairfielder and the Fairfield Diner, which was located across from the post office, where the Brick Walk stands today. It was owned by Artur Guttmann and his wife, Olga, who was known for her Hungarian desserts of Makosh (poppy seed) and Deosh (walnut) rolls. It was a family-run business; Artur's brother-in-law Miki Hirsch also worked for him.

The family was creating a new life in the United States after World War II and the ravages of the Holocaust. Hirsch was born in Czechoslovakia and

The FAIRFIELDER

Serving the finest in Foods 24 hours a day

925 POST ROAD   FAIRFIELD, CONN.

The FAIRFIELDER
925 Post Road -:- Telephone 9-3474

MENU

SANDWICHES

HAMBURGER	20¢
HAMBURGER WITH TOMATO	25¢
CHEESEBURGER	25¢
EGG	20¢
HAM & EGG	35¢
BACON & EGG	35¢
WESTERN	35¢
BOILED HAM	25¢
BACON	25¢
CHEESE	15¢
EGG & CHEESE	25¢
GRILLED HAM	30¢
IMPORTED SWISS CHEESE	25¢
GRILLED CHEESE	25¢
GRILLED HAM & CHEESE	35¢
GRILLED BACON & CHEESE	35¢
TUNA FISH SALAD	35¢
CHICKEN SALAD	35¢
SLICED CHICKEN	60¢
CHICKEN CLUB (3 DECKER)	80¢
LETTUCE & TOMATO	25¢
BACON, LETTUCE & TOMATO	35¢
HAM, LETTUCE & TOMATO	35¢
ALL ROASTED MEAT SANDWICHES	35¢
HOT ROAST BEEF SAND. POT. & VEG.	70¢
HOT TURKEY SAND. POTATO & VEG.	90¢
STEAK SANDWICH (CLOSED)	70¢

Above: In 1955, the Fairfielder Diner was the first establishment to get an official restaurant license from the town of Fairfield. *Courtesy of the Fairfield Museum and History Center.*

Right, top: A hamburger at the Fairfielder cost just twenty cents. *Courtesy of the Fairfield Museum and History Center.*

Right, bottom: Small fry dinners were available for "kiddies" at half price at the Fairfielder. *Courtesy of the Fairfield Museum and History Center.*

The FAIRFIELDER
925 Post Road -:- Telephone 9-3474

MENU
August 14, 1949

JUICES:	
TOMATO, GRAPEFRUIT, PINEAPPLE, ORANGE, PRUNE, APPLE	10¢
SOUP:	
MANHATTAN CLAM CHOWDER	15¢
TODAY'S A LA CARTE SPECIALS:	
BROILED BOSTON BLUE FISH, POTATO & VEGETABLE	85¢
FRIED FILET OF SOLE, POTATO & VEGETABLE	75¢
FRIED DEEP SEA ESCALLOPS, POTATO & VEGETABLE	85¢
BAKED STUFFED CLAMS, & COLE SLAW	55¢
SOFT SHELL CRAB ON TOAST, COLE SLAW & FRENCH FRIES	80¢
FISH CAKES & BEANS	50¢
BAKED MACARONI & CHEESE	60¢
TUNA FISH SALAD PLATE	80¢
LOBSTER SALAD PLATE	95¢
ROAST SIRLOIN OF BEEF, POTATO & VEGETABLE	90¢
ROAST CHICKEN, POTATO & VEGETABLE	85¢
HOT BEEF SANDWICH, POTATO & VEGETABLE	70¢
BRAISED VEAL CUTLET, POTATO & VEGETABLE	80¢
CALVES LIVER & BACON, POTATO & VEGETABLE	95¢
GRILLED PORK CHOPS, POTATO & VEGETABLE	95¢
GRILLED HAM STEAK, POTATO & VEGETABLE	90¢
STEAK SANDWICH, POTATO & VEGETABLE	85¢
SIRLOIN STEAK, POTATO & VEGETABLE	1.80
SMALL FRY DINNERS FOR KIDDIES UP TO 11 YRS. OLD ½ PRICE	
EXCEPT FOR: STEAKS, CHOPS, CUTLETS, HOT SANDWICHES.	
VEGETABLES:	
STEWED TOMATOES, BAKED MACARONI, CARROTS & PEAS, COLE SLAW.	
DESSERTS:	
ASSORTED PIES, LAYER CAKE, POUND CAKE, RAISIN CAKE	10¢
A LA MODE 25¢ ICE CREAM, JELLO, FRUIT CUP, GRAPEFRUIT	
HEARTS, BOSTON CREAM PIE, RICE PUDDING, FRESH APPLE	
SAUCE, WATERMELON, CANTALOUPE, 15¢ A LA MODE 30¢ FRUIT	
BOSTON CREAM PIE 20¢ DESSERTS WITH WHIPPED CREAM 5¢ EXTRA	
BEVERAGES:	
TEA OR COFFEE	10¢
WITH MEALS	05¢
MILK OR CHOCOLATE MILK	12¢
ICED TEA OR COFFEE	10¢
THERE IS AN ADDITIONAL CHARGE OF 5¢ FOR EACH OUTGOING DINNER.	
HOME FRIES WITH ANY ORDER	

was a Holocaust survivor. When the war was over, he was searching for lost family members when he met his wife, also named Olga. They were taken to a displaced persons camp in Cyprus and a year later were allowed to travel to Israel. Hirsch fought in the 1965 Sinai War and then immigrated to United States with his family. After working with Artur, Hirsch wanted to buy his own restaurant and had the opportunity to purchase either the Blue Sky Diner in Bridgeport or the Pike Diner. "He wanted to be closer to home, so he bought the Pike in the '60s," said his daughter, Ruth Neuman. The Pike Diner was one of the first non-Greek diners to open in the area. Located on Black Rock Turnpike, the diner was accessible from both the Merritt Parkway and I-95. It was a place where both locals and out-of-towners could get a good meal and a cup of coffee.

Disaster struck in 1970 when a fire destroyed the building. Each night, the diner would close in the early morning from 2:00 a.m. to 4:00 a.m. for cleaning. One evening, the dishwasher decided to cook pork chops on the grill, which led to the devastating fire.

"It happened to be the best thing," said Neuman. "My father got money to rebuild. He cut out the back and focused on more seating." After the diner was rebuilt, it became a popular place for families who would come in to order the Pike Deluxe hamburger special. "The diner was a way for my parents to make a living and be successful," said Neuman.

The Fairfield Diner was open for business until 1979, when Artur sold it and went into retirement. The building was torn down and replaced by the Brick Walk. The Pike Diner was open until 1982, when it was bought and renamed Penny's II Diner.

Fairfield's Landmark: Larry's Diner

Perhaps Fairfield's most famous diner was Larry's, located on the Post Road. The landmark building was built in 1927 by manufacturer Jerry O'Mahony Inc., the largest dining car factory in the world, based in Elizabeth, New Jersey. The O'Mahony diners were known for their sleek construction. They came in different sizes and styles, but quality and beauty were key elements found in all types. The floors were lined with ceramic tile, and the ceilings were made from Bakelite. The doors were Bakelite or stainless steel, and the side walls were trimmed out in mahogany. Stools lined the bar, and booths lined the windows. A brochure for the cars explained, "A modern Jerry O'Mahony dining car is more than just a casual eating place—it is the kind of place that people enthuse about and return to frequently…Jerry O'Mahony dining cars are recognized by every community as a distinct addition to their particular neighborhood."[102]

One of Fairfield's icons, Larry's Diner was a popular gathering place for over fifty years. *Courtesy of Larry Cultrera.*

Larry's Diner had low wheels and was rolled into town and placed at the corner of the Post Road and Miller Street. Its first owner was Larry Doyle. Originally, the diner had a marble counter where diners could sit and a stand-up bar along the windows. Then in 1936, the diner was moved across the street and was expanded to include booths and more kitchen space. A unique feature was the little picket fence that surrounded the front walk. As was the case with many restaurants of the time, the diner was a family affair. Doyle's son Albert worked alongside his father. In an article from the *Fairfield Citizen*, Albert Doyle recalled his memories of working there as a young boy.

"In those days, you worked 12-hour shifts; we were open 24 hours a day." He washed dishes during his lunch break from grammar school, but he also worked as a counterman, waiter and cook.[103]

In 1941, the diner went under new ownership. According to local legend, Larry Doyle lost the diner in a poker game to an employee named Charles Kadar. That rumor has never been proven, but Kadar and his wife, Catherine, owned the diner for over thirty-eight years. They were no strangers to the restaurant business. Prior to Larry's, they owned the Community Diner in the center of Fairfield and the Beachside Bar at Penfield Beach.

Here, Larry's Diner sits in its second location. It was originally placed directly across the Post Road. *Courtesy of Larry Cultrera.*

They continued to run the diner as a meeting place for locals. They had their "regulars" and handed out small date books at Christmastime. "Larry's Diner in the Heart of Fairfield's Little Times Square," read the title page. "Open Day and Night, Serving—and satisfying, folks with appetites, faithfully for over Twenty Years. Hurry back to Larry's Diner 'Where Everybody Meets Everybody.'"

According to an article from 1975, "There's a cozy, irresistible charm about the gleaming old functional-looking appliances, the marble-topped counter and stained glass windows that have managed to resist change…not to mention the homemade beef stew, goulash, stuffed peppers, cole-slaw, salad, puddings, soups, and generous sandwiches."

The Kadars owned the diner for thirty-five years. Charles died in 2003, and his obituary read, "When interviewed by the *New York Times*, Charlie was asked, 'What famous people came to your diner?' He replied, 'All of my customers are famous.'"[104]

In 1980, the diner was operated by Rita and Konstantinos (Gus) Georgiadis:

Thick coffee cups and heavy green-rimmed plates—Syracuse china—clink as they're set down on a marble counter 50-years-old.

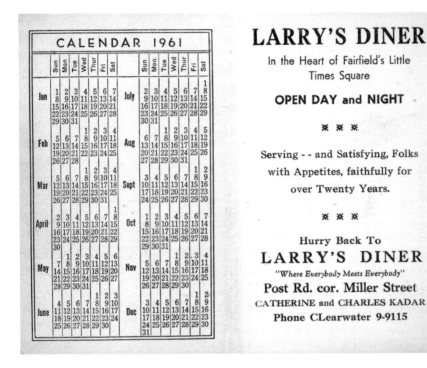

In 1961, the owners of Larry's Diner gave out small datebooks to their customers. Note the location: "In the heart of Fairfield's Little Times Square." *Courtesy of Jim Golias.*

Hamburgers, still called hamburgers, sizzle on a grill, while toast for a triple decker club sandwich pops up in front of an etched glass window in which a lace curtain and a bluebird can dimly be made out. A barreled ceiling, mahogany veneer wood, mirrors between red vinyl benches at chrome and Formica tables, bear no witness to high-tech times. Scenes of Greece cut from a calendar, and on copper plates on the walls, are a current manager's personal touches.

Despite its popularity, this local landmark faced controversy. In 1985, local developer Nicholas Fingelly had plans to construct an office building on the parcel of land where Larry's and two residences stood. The news was devastating to much of the community. The beloved diner where people met for coffee and local gossip since 1927 was about to disappear. People rallied for the diner's preservation.

"The Fairfield Historical Society hopes to be utilized as an advisor for any decision affecting the vintage diner," wrote Nancy P. Serrell in an article from

LITE BITE

Lobster Bisque	350
Soup of the Day	295
Chili	375
Larry's Onion Rings	295
Jumbo Shrimp Cocktail	695
Guacamole with tortilla chips	450
Nachos guacamole, salsa & refried beans	630
Potato Skins with cheddar & bacon	495
Mushroom Caps with snowcrab stuffing & hollandaise	595
Fried Artichoke Hearts with mousseline sauce	450
Baked Brie with seasonal fruit	595
Fried Calamari with hot diavlo sauce	495
Fried Oysters with remoulade sauce	595
Steamed Mussels in white wine & herbs	595

SALADS

Greek Salad feta cheese, bermuda onion, cucumber, anchovies, tomato, olives & oregano, with mixed greens, served with oil & vinegar	595
Tostada Salad refried beans, salsa, bleu olives, tomato & avocado on a corn tortilla with melted cheddar, served with sour cream & guacamole	595
Chef Salad julienned ham, turkey, swiss, american cheese, egg & tomato wedges	695
Curried Chicken Salad chicken, apples & scallions in a mild curry sauce, served with chutney & fresh vegetables	695
Cobb Salad heart of avocado, turkey, bacon, tomato, egg & gorgonzola cheese	695
Mediterranean Seafood Salad marinated mix of scungilli, calamari, shrimp & scallops	795
Spinach Salad egg, bacon, bermuda onion, fresh croutons & mushrooms	595
Aztec Salad shrimp sautéed with jalapeños, onions, tomatoes, olives & garlic, served over cool salad greens, sprinkled with cheddar cheese, in a flour tortilla topped with guacamole	1095

ENTREES

All Entrees served with the house salad & choice of baked potato, rice or fries

Roast Prime Rib of Beef au jus	1395
Chesapeake Chicken chicken breasts stuffed with mushrooms, swiss, sautéed peppers & snowcrab, served with hollandaise	1395
Baked Stuffed Shrimp in a casserole with snowcrab stuffing	1495
Louisiana Chicken marinated in buttermilk, seasoned with 14 herbs & spices, deep fried	1195
Fresh Lobster steamed, baked-stuffed or broiled	Market
Grilled Pork Chops	1295
Grilled Lamb Chops marinated in anise & garlic	1695
Grilled Rib Eye Steak	1495
Spicy Grilled Marinated Shrimp & Scallop Kabob	1495
Sautéed Calves' Liver with bacon, onions & avocado	1195

PASTAS

All served with the house salad

Fettuccini Alfredo with mushrooms, bacon or gorgonzola, add any or all three · Each Item 100	1095
Steamed Cherrystones over Linguini steamed in herb butter & wine or in fra diavlo sauce	1195
Tortellini Primavera cheese filled pasta, sautéed with a garden of fresh vegetables, herbs & pignoli nuts	1095
Spinach Fettuini, Artichoke Hearts & Tomato with mushrooms & fine herbs in a light cream sauce & parmesan cheese	1095
Pasta, Shrimp & Broccoli sautéed in garlic oil, topped with parmesan	1395
Straw & Hay spinach fettuini & linguini with smoked ham & peas, sautéed in a light tomato cream sauce, topped with parmesan	1195
Mussels over Linguini steamed in garlic, herbs & wine or in fra diavlo sauce	1095
Shrimp Marinara or Fra Diavlo over linguini	1495

Ask about our Blue Plate
and our Diner Dess

SANDWICHES & BURGERS

Chicken Salad in a pita	595
Sliced Prime Rib au jus on a dub roll	795
Turkey, Bacon & Avocado Melt served on a croissant with lettuce & tomato	695
Liverwurst, Bermuda Onion & Tomato with a creamy horseradish sauce on black bread	595
Smoked Ham & Melted Vermont Cheddar with champagne mustard on multi-grain bread	595
Build Your Own Burger add swiss, american, cheddar, or mozzarella cheese, bacon, chili, mushrooms or guacamole · Each Item 30	495

The above are served with fries, slaw & pickle

SIDES

Fries	225
Sautéed Mushroom	295
Cole Slaw	175
Vegetable of the Day	230
	230
	200

Over the years, the menu at Larry's Diner evolved to include upscale entrées such as fresh lobster and fettuccini Alfredo. *Courtesy of Alison Healy.*

1985. "Society curator Chris Nevins sees Larry's as 'a 1920s or '30s version of the Sun Tavern,' worthy of preservation as a meaningful landmark in Fairfield's history."

The developer assured residents that he didn't want to see the diner endangered or desecrated in any way. Talk swirled around the idea of donating the diner to the Smithsonian Museum, but it was absolutely clear that the diner had to go elsewhere.

As it turned out, the Smithsonian wasn't exactly chomping at the bit for a little slice of Fairfield's history. Fingelly sold the diner (for an undisclosed amount) to restaurateurs Ross Proctor, co-owner of the Elm City Diner in New Haven, and Philip DeStefano, co-owner of Thatcher's restaurant in Darien. While the pair planned their new venture, the diner was temporarily housed in a storage space that the town provided for free as part of its contribution toward the diner's preservation.

The plan was to connect the diner to a two-story restaurant at 55 Miller Street. The original coffee cup sign would hang over the bar area, and the restaurant would be named Larry's.[105] The new incarnation of Larry's didn't last long, however, and soon became a southwestern restaurant named Rattlesnake Bar & Grill. From there, it became an

Italian restaurant called Mulino's, which closed in 2007. And that's when things really changed.

The new owner, Vincente Siguenza, had plans for an Italian restaurant called 55 Wine Bar—and his plans didn't include a diner aesthetic. This time, there was no public outcry. The original wooden doors from Larry's were utilized in the second-floor dining room while the car itself was dismantled to create space for an outdoor patio. Larry's is now but a memory.

The Walls Have Ears

Chances are if you were out past midnight, perhaps dancing at nearby Fredericksburg, and needed an egg sandwich on a hard roll, you stopped at the Green Comet Diner. Local teenagers had their own special moniker for it—the Green Vomit, although the name wasn't fitting. The silver and green diner was one of the most popular spots in town.

Opened in 1940 by Knute Lindfors and Harold Erickson, the diner was ideally situated off of Exit 24 on I-95 on King's Highway Cutoff. Truckers would often stop there for a quick meal. Local humor/gossip columnist Harry Neigher often wrote about the goings-on at the diner, such as this tidbit: "A waitress at the Green Comet was bragging to a customer, 'I have my mother's eyes, my mother's nose and my mother's mouth.' 'Gee,' replied the wise-gee [sic], 'that must leave your mother with a pretty vacant expression.'"[106]

All joking aside, the Green Comet apparently was a great place to work. Shirley Burr was a waitress there from 1955 to 1975. "There wasn't ever a person who could ever say anything about [Lindfors and Erickson] because everybody liked them," she was quoted as saying in an article from 2005. "You couldn't get a job there when I was there," she said. "The Green Comet was the very best."

In fact, it was such a great place to work that it was made mention of in several obituaries. Stergios Koutikas started at the Green Comet in 1973 as a dishwasher before opening his own restaurant—the New Colony Diner—in 1976.[107] Bertha Erdoss, who lived to be 105 years old, worked for many years as a waitress there,[108] as did Elsie Byrd, who put in 25 years of service.[109]

Eventually, the diner was sold and became known as the Eldorado Diner. Then in 1993, the Eldorado was sold to the Anthis family, who kept it as a diner but with one radical change: they introduced a vegetarian menu.

The Fairfield Diner & Vegetarian Enclave offered a unique combination of typical hearty diner fare (read: lots of bacon and sausage) and meatless dishes like grilled polenta, veggie burgers and falafel.[110] They were known for their creative menu but became newsworthy when a corruption scandal involving Bridgeport mayor Joseph Ganim hit the news. As part of the investigation, it was learned that FBI agents bugged the diner, which was frequented by several individuals involved in the scandal.[111] The notoriety didn't seem to affect the diner, though. If anything, it attracted more visitors. The diner was open for twelve years before the lease to the property was sold to Lexus of Westport, a car dealership next door.[112]

8

SPICING THINGS UP

Kuhn's Corner

If Gasper Kuhn is to be remembered for anything, it would be his work ethic. And his roast beef. And, oh yeah, the chili. And don't forget the Hungarian food.

A foreman at Sikorsky in the 1940s, Kuhn wasn't content to just work his shift as a foreman and then go home. Driven by a powerful sense of accomplishment and hard work, Kuhn decided to open a restaurant in 1946 on the corner of Black Rock Turnpike and Tunxis Hill Cutoff. This was in the days before McDonald's, long before the Black Rock Turnpike began to see development. Kuhn's hot dog stand was one of a kind and drew people from all over. The menu was simple: hot dogs, burgers, fries and sodas. "In the '40s, people would be coming up in Cadillacs and Packards," said Richard Kuhn, one of Gasper's five children. "People would line up out the door," he said. "There would be thirty or forty people lined up out the door all the time, rain or shine. The line started at ten and didn't end until two."[113]

Richard and his brothers, Keith, Ronnie and Roger, worked at Kuhn's hot dog stand from a young age. "We were six, seven years old," said Richard. The boys were tasked with a variety of jobs, from sweeping and cleaning to peeling potatoes.

"Back then, the fries weren't frozen," said Richard. "We used to peel them, cut them, blanch them and fry them." They would go through thousands of pounds of potatoes a week.

Long before the fork of Black Rock Turnpike and Tunxis Hill became a congested traffic byway, the land was mostly use for farming. In this photo from the 1940s, the original Kuhn's restaurant was the only place around to get a quick meal. *Courtesy of the Kuhn family.*

Business was particularly brisk in the summer, when an area known as Gypsy Springs became populated by Hungarian campers.

The hot dog stand stood on a huge tract of land that included an old gas station. In 1950, Gasper converted the gas station into a full-service restaurant, with sit-down dining and restrooms. "The original restaurant was forty by twenty feet," said Richard. "The kitchen was twelve by eight feet." The Kuhn brothers recalled that there was a service table with two drawers, a dishwasher, a meat slicer, an eight-burner stove, a fryolater and a steam table.

Everything on the menu was homemade. "We were best known for our roast beef sandwiches," said Roger. "But we also had ham, meatloaf, kielbasa, homemade soups." Kuhn's proximity to the Hungarian side of town was evident in their Wednesday specials: chicken paprikash and stuffed cabbage.

As the boys got older, their duties at the restaurant increased. "We cooked, served, bar tended," said Roger. Perhaps one of their least favorite jobs was

A hardworking man, Gasper Kuhn went from being a foreman at Sikorsky's to owning Kuhn's, a Fairfield landmark for over fifty years. *Courtesy of Keith Kuhn.*

cleaning up the outside. "We had a broom handle with a nail on the end," said Roger. "We'd use it to pick up papers and cigarettes."

"There had to be dozens of garbage cans around the restaurant," said Keith. "But it was a different time. People didn't understand littering. We'd have to clean up after them. The broom stick was passed on from brother to brother." Even Gasper's grandson Roger remembers having "stick duty."

Times were good, and Gasper expanded the restaurant. The majority of the addition extended the bar room. Kuhn's became a hugely popular neighborhood restaurant, with generations of families coming in for dinner. The roast beef was a huge draw.

"We cooked 500 to 750 pounds of roast beef a week," said Roger. "It was cooked, cooled, refrigerated, sliced, then put in a big tray filled with gravy."

"The gravy was the secret," said Keith. The roast beef was then served on rye bread, a hard roll or a grinder. But it wasn't just the roast beef that made mouths water.

Kuhn's quickly became famous locally for its chili. According to Richard, Gasper had a friend from Texas who introduced him to a chili recipe. From there, Gasper tweaked it.

"When people think of chili, they often think of it as something you eat out of a bowl," said Keith. "Kuhn's chili is a condiment." Most notably, of course, as a topping for their hot dogs. "Everyone tries to duplicate the recipe," said Keith. "It's very spicy but it has flavor. Anybody can make anything hot, but you have to have flavor and good body."

What's the secret to Kuhn's famous chili? "Unless you marry into the family, you'll never know," said Keith. "We like to say, 'A little bit of this, a little bit of that, some of this, some of that.'" But in fact, there is a science to the recipe. "You cannot deviate," said Richard. "One time I made it, and

I didn't measure ingredients. I thought, 'What's the difference?' My father wanted to kill me."

Today, Keith still makes the chili for retail sale. It's sold by the quart at the Five-O Food Store on Black Rock Turnpike and is used at Danny's Drive-In in Stratford, Captain's Cove in Bridgeport and the Windmill in Stratford.

C.B. Cebulski, a writer and editor for Marvel comics, described his love for Kuhn's chili on his blog, "Eataku." He wrote:

> *My father and grandfather both ate at Kuhn's and I have fond childhood memories of going for hot dogs there with them when I was growing up. Kuhn's was actually right across the street from the five and dime I bought my comics at when I was a kid. And the one thing that made them famous was their chili. It was spicy hot with this exquisite, fragrant flavor. Kuhn's chili packed that 'good heat,' one that you enjoyed; it brought a burn that you didn't immediately wash away with a cold drink as you wanted to savor that fiery sensation in your mouth. Packed with onions, their chili just coated the hot dogs and soaked into the buns for an incredible eating experience. I couldn't handle it when I was really young, but came to love it as I grew up and my taste buds expanded. It was unique, unlike any chili I have ever had to this day.*"[114]

Talking with the Kuhn brothers about the restaurant is a trip down memory lane, with each story snowballing into the next. They tell of the time a blizzard hit and nothing in town was open. Gasper walked to the restaurant to check on things, and someone knocked on the door looking for food. Then came another visitor and then another. Before long, the bar was full, and the kitchen was wiped out of all the bread, rolls and milk.

At one point, when Gasper was having repeated problems with the refrigerator, he decided to take matters into his own hands. Rather than continuing to pay for a repairman, he signed up for a night course in refrigerator repair at Bullard Havens.

As the brothers share their stories, they continually repeat the importance of family. "Our customers were family, in the best sense of the word," said Roger. "My father taught us that family was always very important."

Despite the consistent success and local fame of Kuhn's, things changed in the 1980s. The population of the town was booming, and Black Rock Turnpike was undergoing massive retail growth. Gasper was getting too old to run the restaurant, and he was made an offer he couldn't refuse. Kuhn's closed in 1987, and a shopping center now stands in its place.

9
OTTAVIO'S

Politics and Parties

When it came to finding locations to host special events in Fairfield, the choices were few. In the early 1960s, the Fairfield Motor Inn operated as both a restaurant and a banquet hall for special occasions. The restaurant was divided into four sections: the Champagne Dining Room, the Black Watch room, the Carnival room and the Mandarin Lounge. The décor was anything but subtle: floor-to-ceiling drapes shaded from red to orange; deep-colored, inlaid enamel panels on the walls set off with grapes and dried foliage painted gold.[115] During the day, the restaurant offered a lunch buffet that included "three hot dishes, platters of sliced ham, turkey and roast beef, assorted seafood and vegetable salads, relish-topped eggs" and more. In her review, columnist Barbara Graham wrote, "Noontimes this restaurant is well populated with executives who linger over coffee. Toward the shank of the afternoon, come the cocktailers to the snug Mandarin Lounge and you will note that the drinks prepared here are well mixed and served and definitely of the variety which is known as 'king sized.'"[116] The Fairfield Motor Inn was able to accommodate up to three hundred guests for private functions. Nearby, Frederick's was a popular choice for weddings, and there were various organizations like the VFW and the Elks Club that had space available for parties. But the swankiest place for weddings, bar mitzvahs and celebrations was Ottavio's on Post Road.

Otto Veglio grew up in "the Hollow" in Bridgeport, a mostly Italian neighborhood.[117] "I remember on Sunday mornings, my mother would send me for bread," he said. "All you could smell walking there was sauce. I'd go get the bread and I'd start eating it on the way home." Later, he moved to the North End, which had a large Irish, Italian and Jewish population. He began working in the catering business, and from there his career took off.

Veglio got a job as a manager at the Fairfield Motor Inn and worked there for a year when he found out the restaurant was going to close. He got the idea that he was going to open his own catering business. In order to get a vision of what he wanted, he took a job at Astoria Manor in Long Island, a popular, glitzy banquet hall, and kept his eye on every part of the business. When Veglio was looking for a spot to create his catering business, he looked at the former First National Supermarket in the heart of downtown on the Post Road but couldn't afford the lease price. Unbeknownst to him, the owners were related to his wife. "Frank Carroll [one of the owners] said, 'Don't worry about it. We can make a deal,'" said Veglio. "He was the kind of guy who shook your hand when he made a promise, and he kept it."

On May 27, 1963, what had once been a supermarket filled with aisles of boxes and cans reopened as the town's ritziest banquet hall—Ottavio's, named after Veglio's father. After a remodeling job that cost over $100,000, the former grocery store was converted into a twelve-thousand-foot red-carpeted facility with accommodations for up to seven hundred diners.[118]

Before the building even opened, Veglio already had seventeen parties booked. They were people who had events scheduled at the Fairfield Motor Inn, which was getting ready to close. That spot then became the Rustic Grotto, a dark cave-like restaurant with an Italian-themed menu. One regular customer recalled the stuffed mushrooms. "I'd never heard that you could stuff a mushroom before, and they were so delicious," he said. "The Grotto was the first real restaurant I remember going to." In the 1970s, the Grotto (as it came to be known) had a bustling bar scene. In 1996, the Rustic Grotto was sold and became the Circle Diner, which is still here today.

Ottavio's was decked out in a Mediterranean theme, and fold away partitions divided the dining area into four separate rooms. Potential clients were given a red velveteen menu. Imprinted on the cover in gold it read, "Ottavio's: Excellence Is Our Mark of Distinction."

Each meal would start with hors d'oevures, followed by manicotti or antipasto, sherbet and an entrée: lobster tails, surf and turf, roast beef, prime rib, filet mignon, boneless stuffed chicken, poulet au champagne, chicken francaise, veal milanase, veal francaise or veal cordon bleu. "We did everything New York style," said Veglio. "Fairfield never saw a Venetian table until I brought it in," he said. In addition to a spread of desserts, another option for parties was the Candy Man—a waiter who would offer

Lunch Menu

FRUIT CUP	1.00
JUMBO SHRIMP COCKTAIL	4.25
CLAMS ON HALF SHELL	3.25

ZUPPA DEL GIORNO   INCLUDED with the FOLLOWING

- ANTIPASTO 3.50
- CHEF SALAD a la GROTTO 3.95
- SPAGHETTI or LINGUINE MARINARA 3.75
- SPAGHETTI or LINGUINE with CLAM SAUCE
  RED or WHITE 4.95
- SPAGHETTI with MEATBALLS 4.25
- LASAGNA al FORNO 4.25
- MUSSELS POSILLUPO with LINGUINE . . 4.25
- LONDON BROIL a la GROTTO 4.95
- CHICKEN PARMIGIANA al FORNO . . 4.50
- VEAL PARMIGIANA al FORNO 4.95
- CHOPPED SIRLOIN on bun with FRENCH FRIES 3.25
- OPEN STEAK SANDWICH with FRENCH FRIES . 4.95
- HOT CORNED BEEF with CHEESE/FRENCH FRIES . 3.50
- HOT PASTRAMI with CHEESE/FRENCH FRIES . 3.50
- FILET OF SOLE BROILED 4.50

TOSSED SALAD....75
CHEESE DRESSING..45   GARLIC BREAD... 1.00

Italian fare was the focus of the menu at the Grotto, the restaurant adjacent to the Fairfield Motor Inn. *Courtesy of Sue Steele.*

lemon ice and a cart full of candy while Sammy Davis Jr.'s "The Candy Man" played over the speakers.

One of Veglio's first events was a stag party for his nephew. The dishwasher hadn't arrived yet, and Veglio panicked. He asked Jack Rudis, who owned the restaurant Rudy's about a quarter of a mile away, what he should do. "Jack said, 'Bring the dishes to me. I'll clean them.'" So the waitstaff shuttled the dishes down to Rudy's. "Jack washed every dish, cup, saucer and spoon," said Veglio.

Large entrées were a trademark of the Grotto Restaurant. *Courtesy of Sue Steele.*

The opening of Ottavio's meant a lot of job opportunities for the local teenagers. When Tony Danforth was in high school, he got a job as a dishwasher. "I'd work weekends until 1 a.m.," he said.[119] "Washing dishes was constant. We got so good at handling plates we could grab three plates at once using our fingers. I remember they would always play, 'Sh Boom (Life Could Be a Dream).' As we washed dishes, we could hear the music."

Lewis Chappell and his brother Rob also had jobs as dishwashers. "We would work for twelve-plus hours," he said. "We'd be paid cash at the end

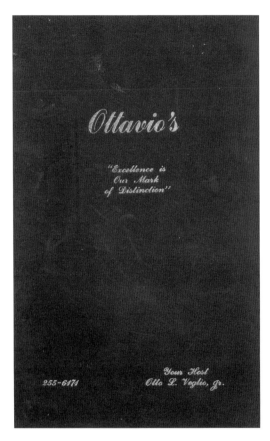

Ottavio's

"*Excellence is Our Mark of Distinction*"

255-6171

Your Host Otto L. Veglio, jr.

When planning a wedding reception or anniversary party, Ottavio's was the place to go in Fairfield. The red velvet menu hinted at the classic Italian décor of the catering hall. *Courtesy of Dr. Gladys Gress.*

of the night. Otto taught us great work ethics."[120]

It seemed as if every group and organization held their parties at Ottavio's. Veglio got hooked in with Fairfield University, Sacred Heart University, the Chamber of Commerce and many local clubs. "My first real big break was Stewart McKinney's campaign party for 450 people," said Veglio. "I was a nervous wreck." But with the proper planning, Veglio was able to serve 450 filet mignon dinners in under eighteen minutes.

That was just the start of the political dinners that Veglio would host. When Rosalyn Carter was in town, he provided dinners for 850 people at the University of Bridgeport. There weren't any stoves or refrigerators at the facility, so all the food had to be warmed and carted there. When Ronald Reagan visited Fairfield, Veglio provided meals for the entourage.

But it wasn't the famous people that Veglio remembers most. Rather, it was the charitable functions that have stayed with him all these years. "We did a dinner once to raise money for a young girl who needed a heart operation. There were over four hundred people there. Fifteen years went by, and we were doing a wedding. The bride said her maid of honor wanted to do a toast. She came up and stood next to me and asked everybody to toast me. She was the girl with the heart. I had no idea." In addition, he recalled dinners that he did two times a year for local needy children. But perhaps the biggest event that occurred at Ottavio's was Veglio's daughter's wedding.

"We had a tent in the parking lot with a two-piece band," he recalled. "There were two thousand American Beauty roses on each side of the bandstand. There were five hundred geraniums, floral roping and blue gardenias floating in bowls on the tables. We had a horse and carriage bring the bridal party down the Post Road from the Sherman Green. After the wedding, we had a chuck wagon breakfast in the parking lot."

Not every wedding was as spectacular, but Ottavio's was the place for a glamourous celebration. Melanie Stewart recalled that her mother chose Ottavio's for her wedding reception. "It was very, you know, Italian," she said. "It was a very nice reception. We had stuffed chicken. People still talk about my reception, and my husband and I aren't even together anymore."[121]

For Veglio, running the business was all about the people. "We wanted to offer it all—ambiance, food, service. We let them know that they were the king and queen for the day."

In 1993, Ottavio's closed, leaving future brides to seek other places for the ultimate wedding reception. Veglio went on to work in the hotel business, and the Ottavio's building was torn down. Today, the site is home to a pharmacy.

THE LITTLE RESTAURANT THAT COULD

Dining Out on Commerce Drive

Long before Pepe's moved onto Commerce Drive, before the post office and the Porsche dealership became milestones, this area of town was solitary. A mix of industrial, businesses and residences, it wasn't a place you'd go to unless you had a reason.

But on that stretch of road was a little building that would withstand all of the changes of time.

In the 1970s, a small cinderblock building housed the Beer Mug, a neighborhood bar with jukebox.

"The Beer Mug wasn't much of a place," said Howard Meyer. "It was a bar and a pool table."[122] The interior was painted mustard yellow and two bare lightbulbs descended from the ceiling. Yet Meyer saw something in that tiny place. He had a vision. In 1982, Meyer and his business partner Peter Lyddy decided to buy it and call it Chadwix.

"Everyone told us we were crazy because that section of town wasn't developed," he said. But the pair, who were both working at the Peppermill restaurant in Westport at the time, had an idea.

"In December 1982 we opened," Meyer said. "We only had beer and wine, so we did a good lunch business, but not a good dinner service." Chadwix was one of two establishments in Fairfield that operated under a tavern permit. The other was the Button Ball Tavern. At the time, Fairfield's zoning laws stipulated that two businesses within 1,500 feet of each other could not have the same liquor permit. Nearby, Ana Capri, an Italian restaurant, had a full-service bar permit, so Chadwix was out of luck. Fortunately, zoning

CHADWIX
OF FAIRFIELD

NACHOS . . 6.25

SOUPS CUP BOWL

French ONION . . . 1.75 3.50
Chili 1.93 3.95
Soup du Jour . . . 1.75 3.50

SALADS

According to Eighteenth Century gastronome, Jean Anthelme Brillat-Savarin, a salad "freshens without enfeebling and fortifies without irritating."

Chef Meats & cheeses abound in this hefty garden feast 6.50
Spinach with crisp bacon & quartered eggs generously laced throughout 5.50
House A bounty of fresh garden delights 3.95
Salad Salads Tuna or egg prepared platter style 6.25

BURGERS

A sandwich consists of such meat placed between the halves of a rand roll ... & then some!
Plain & Simple Prime beef char-broiled the way you like it 4.50
Cheese Your choice... American, Swiss, Cheddar or Bleu 4.95
Bacon Cheese Combine your choice of cheese & crispy bacon strips 5.25
Chili A three alarm burger not to be passed up 4.95
Mushroom A heaping helping of our super mushroom sauce sits atop this burger . . 4.95
Diet Minus the roll & garnished to the dieter's delight 4.75
Chadwix Our plain & simple burger with all the above toppings 5.95

HOT DOGS

A weenie extended to a foot long & topped with the trappings that make this old standard a meal!
Plain & Simple Alone on a roll or with mustard, relish & sauerkraut 3.50
The Trappings Chili, bacon or cheese (.40¢ each)
Chadwix Another special sauce from our chef to really extend the flavor of this dog.
Served with french fries 4.25

SANDWICHES

John Montagu, 4th Earl of Sandwich (1718-1792), who is said to be the originator, would be proud of these selections! Following served on white, light rye, dark rye or hard roll —

Corned Beef	4.95	Pastrami	4.95	Egg Salad	4.25	Turkey	4.95
Roast Beef	4.95	Ham	4.95	Tuna Salad	4.50

CHADWICHES

Monte Cristo Swiss & ham & turkey on french toast 5.75
Grilled Cheese Grilled American, Cheddar or Swiss 3.95
Chadwix Melt Hamburger patty tucked inside our grilled cheese 4.95
Steak Sandwich N.Y. Strip with sauteed onions, melted Swiss on a hard roll w/french fries . 6.95
Club A triple decker of bacon, lettuce, tomato & turkey or ham, or roast beef 5.75
Hot Roast Beef Roast beef served open face on rye bread topped with gravy . . . 5.25
Tuna Melt Fresh tuna served open face on rye bread with bacon and melted cheese 5.25
Reuben Corned beef & Swiss grilled together w/ sauerkraut & Russian dressing . . 5.25
B-B-Q Beef Roast beef sauteed in BBQ sauce on a hard roll with french fries . . 5.25

SIDE DISHES

French Fries 1.00   Coleslaw 1.00   Cottage Cheese 1.00

· See blackboard for Daily Specials ·   · Eastern Standard Time Brunch Served ·

In the 1980s, menus started to feature more salads and sandwiches and fewer entrées. Chadwix was known for its popular burgers. *Courtesy of Howard Meyer.*

laws changed, and Chadwix was able to secure a full liquor license. "We became very active. There was a lot of money flowing around."

Today, over 80 percent of restaurant bills are charged to debit, credit or pre-paid cards. This makes the dining experience easier for patrons, but it's a mixed bag for restaurant owners. Contrast that with the '80s. Certainly some people paid their restaurant bills with Diners Club cards, which were first released in 1950, but the majority of people paid cash.[123]

"What happens now," said Meyer, "on a Saturday night, the owner ends up with negative cash. When people put tips on plastic, the owner has to tip out his waitstaff, and the credit card reimbursement doesn't come until Tuesday." Meyer said he wouldn't own a restaurant today because the cost of food is so high. New York strip, which used to sell for two dollars a pound, now sells for nine dollars a pound. Scallops could be gotten for three dollars a pound, now they run around fifteen dollars. "You just can't generate enough capital to run a restaurant," Meyer said.

Things were certainly different in the '80s. From 1979 to 1989, the top industry adding the most jobs in the service sector were eating and drinking establishments. Within that decade, jobs in the restaurant sector rose 41.1 percent.[124] But the differences weren't just economic.

"The biggest difference between now and then," said Meyer, "was that people went out to lunch while they were working. They'd have a couple of martinis, a glass of Sambuca with their coffee." Meyer said they would open at 11:30 a.m. for lunch and people would continue to come in until 2:30 p.m., cutting into the dinner hour. "Back in the '80s, we served a lot of alcohol at lunch. It's not a good thing, but DUI's were much more tolerable then."

A SPRINKLE OF STARDUST

Meyer said the patrons were a mixed Fairfield crowd, ranging from young to old, blue-collar workers to businessmen. "We had a bunch of old-timers who would come three times a week right at 11:30 because they wanted the corner table. I like to say we were a sports bar before there were sports bars."

The menu at Chadwix was classic and comfortable. There were salads—chef, tossed, with tuna or egg salad; roast beef, turkey and ham sandwiches; gourmet burgers; and hot dogs. There were always chicken, beef and seafood specials. The restaurant was repeatedly awarded Best Nachos in Fairfield County by the local entertainment newspaper.

Howard Meyer took a chance on a tiny building on Commerce Drive and created Chadwix, one of the most popular restaurants/bars in Fairfield in the 1980s. *Courtesy of Howard Meyer.*

"The kitchen was open until midnight seven days a week," said Meyer. "We had a very strong late night presence. A lot of diners were restaurant workers. They knew they could come in at 11:00 after their shift and get a full meal."

One of Meyer's favorite memories was in 1985 when Hurricane Gloria hit. On September 28, the Category 2 storm hit, wreaking havoc on area homes and businesses. Most of the town was out of power. Due to its location adjacent to the railroad tracks, however, Chadwix was one of the first places to have its power restored. Somehow word got out that the tiny restaurant was open for business.

"There was a four-and-a-half-hour wait for dinner," said Meyer. "People said, 'We'll wait.' They lined up in front with cocktails in hand. We served our last meal at twenty to two that night."

In 1989, Denise Collette took over the tiny space and reimagined it as Tucker's Café. There was seating for about three dozen people and another ten spaces at the bar. She had no idea that the area was about to undergo major changes. First came BJ's Wholesale Club in 1990 and then came the Showcase Cinemas in Bridgeport and Fairfield Cinemas at Bullard Square, which all brought traffic and attention to the area. "When the movie theaters moved in, it was like God sprinkled stardust on me," said Collette.[125]

The menu at Tucker's continued along the same classic, comfortable lines as Chadwix. Burgers and sandwiches were popular, and entrées were heavily seafood-based. One regular item was the seafood chowder with chunks of lobster, shrimp and scallops. Collette modeled the recipe on the chowder that was served at the nearby Ships restaurant in Westport. In the winter, the menu's focus switched to comfort foods like meatloaf, beef stew and shepherd's pie. Tucker's was open for twenty-four years before it closed in 2013. And just as all things come full-circle, she sold the business to Tommy Febbraio—former owner of the Scenario, Tommy's and Sidetracks, three of Fairfield's most beloved lost restaurants. Today, it is known as the Little Goose.

TUCKER'S HOME-STYLE BEEF STEW[126]

2 pounds lean stew meat
2 carrots, sliced
1 Spanish onion, diced
4 celery stalks, diced
2 cloves garlic, chopped
1 large can plum tomatoes, chopped
3 cups beef stock
2 bay leaves
4 potatoes cubed

In a large pot, sauté stew meat in 2 tablespoons of oil or butter. Cook until beef is lightly browned. Add carrots, onion and celery and cook for 3 minutes until veggies are tender. Add garlic and tomatoes and cook for another 3 minutes. Stir in beef stock, bay leaves and potatoes and bring to boil. Reduce heat and simmer for 1½ hours. Stir occasionally and add water if necessary. You can leave stew covered and standing for another hour to allow the beef to become more tender and all the flavors to really blend. This is a great dish if having company because you can make it the day before and just heat it up before you want to serve. Warm crusted bread and a salad are great compliments to this meal.

ꟼHE 1970ꜱ

Changing Tastes

When the beloved Center Restaurant closed, people wondered what would take its place. They didn't have to question it for too long. The restaurant was bought by two young entrepreneurs fresh out of college, Thomas Febbraio and Matthew Senie. The pair gutted the restaurant and loosely combined their last names to create "the Scenario," a restaurant they hoped would cater to commuters and professionals, as well as those interested in entertainment. "We had plays up on top," said Febbraio, who now owns several restaurants and is in the commercial real estate business.[127] "It was more like a dinner theater. People thought of us as a playhouse." The restaurant featured entertainment ranging from off-Broadway dramas and stand-up comedy to '50s musical revues and children's theater.

It was wildly popular for a time, but eventually, Febbraio said, "The model wasn't working, so I bought my partner out." That's when he brought in another partner, Thomas Sargent. "It was reborn as Tommy's," said Febbraio. "We didn't do plays, although on weekends we had a piano player upstairs." The bar was a lively meeting place. Photographs of famous Toms, like Tom Selleck and Thomas Edison, adorned the walls, and eventually a few video games drew in groups of friends. "It was a very active bar crowd," said Febbraio. "It was like a Cheers. Everyone had their own seat, including Harry Reasoner." The famous television journalist lived in nearby Westport and was just one famous face that frequented Tommy's. "Oprah was there twice, Phil Donahue, Michael Bolton, Rod Stewart [and] Pamela Anderson."

After the Center Restaurant closed, Tommy Febbraio opened the Scenario, a restaurant and bar where cabaret-style performances were held in the upstairs dining room. *Courtesy of Elly and Lorry Scott.*

The menu at Tommy's was rich and indulgent, like the 1980s themselves. Favorites on the menu included shrimp and chicken Amalfi, which was served in a garlic brandy sauce. Veal bundles were another favorite.

Febbraio said that the menu is a time capsule of a more decadent era. "Kids today eat totally different," he said. "It's all about shared and small. It used to be you'd sit down at a table with a white tablecloth and order an appetizer and a salad and a main course. Now, rather than sitting down and having a four-course dinner, it's a totally different concept today."

Febbraio acknowledged that his staff was a big reason for the restaurant's success. "The staff never seemed to leave," he said.

Ed Waiksnis recalled his memories of the waitstaff at Tommy's. He used to work the door at Archie Moore's, a restaurant located behind Tommy's. "The waitstaff from Tommy's would duck out, come down the alley, get shots at Archie's, then go back down the alley and back to waiting on their tables at Tommy's."[128]

Tommy's had been the center of the Fairfield social scene for twenty-five years when Febbraio decided it was time to call it quits. "I got tired of being in the same place," he said. He sold the restaurant to Easton residents Martin Ferrari and Kostas Brillis, who turned the restaurant into the short-lived Rooster's, which had more of a diner feel.[129] "When I closed Tommy's, I probably received over two hundred letters from people."

On the Corner

Febbraio, however, was not out of the Fairfield restaurant scene entirely because on Valentine's Day 1985, during the height of Tommy's heyday, he opened Sidetracks. Named because of its location adjacent to the railroad tracks, Sidetracks was just one of a number of restaurants that occupied the space on the corner of the Post Road and North Pine Creek over the years.

In the 1800s, the corner building served as a saloon for travelers passing though from New York to Boston. In 1936, Jack Rudis opened Rudy's Restaurant; it was the first place in town to get a liquor license after Prohibition ended. There, one could get a roast beef dinner or corned beef and cabbage for twenty-five cents. A glass of Old Overholt whiskey was the same price. A sign on the side of the building advertised "Bar-B-Frank: Oven Roasted Franks. Sanitized. Greaseless."[130]

An advertisement in a local phone directory pointed out there was dancing every evening. Wednesday night was cocktail night and every Thursday was amateur night.

In 1964, Joe Sepot, who was having success down at the bottom of South Pine Creek Road with his bar Surfside, opened Papa Schultz's, a restaurant specializing in German fare and boasting an oompah band, in the spot where Rudy's had been.[131] The restaurant stayed open for two years. In 1966, it became Ward's Steak House until 1968. And the restaurant kept changing. From 1968 to 1973, it was open as the Black Horse Tavern.

From 1973 to 1976, it was the Greek-themed Acropolis, an exotic addition to Fairfield's otherwise mostly continental dining scene. Not only was the food new and different—things like pastichio, moussaka, spanakopita and dolmathes—but they also had a belly dancer performing on weekend nights. A review in the *Connecticut Sunday Herald* alluded to the slightly suggestive goings-on: "A sinous, well-endowed exotic dancer from Morocco, Varinia, slithered amongst the tables last weekend…Excited diners, following Grecian custom, smashed five plates on the floor in tribute."[132] The owners, Maury Bassler and Peter Chirigos, hoped to bring a little piece of Greece to Fairfield. The Acropolis was the only restaurant in the state that featured a whole baby lamb roasted on a five-foot-long rotisserie spit specialy imported from Athens. The reviewer wrote, "When the Acropolis opened, the Greek chef was serving the roast lamb a la Grecque, which means with bones in it. Americans were horrified; they didn't realize this meat is the sweetest. Now they are asked if they prefer lamb on or off the bone." It was going to take a bit of time for Fairfielders to adapt to this new cuisine. The article made note of the restaurant's other "unusual piece of gourmet equipment," the gyros. "This is a tall, up-ended roaster around which is packed a mixture of three different kinds of chopped meat. The meat is slowly rotated, and when crisp, sliced off and eaten sandwiched between pieces of pita, Greek bread." The author continued, "This is known as a souvlaki sandwich, and is rapidly replacing the hot dog on stands throughout Manhattan. It's all the rage." Souvlaki never did replace the hot dog, and the Acropolis didn't make it in Fairfield. It closed in 1976. For a brief year following, the location was known as the Double J, a country western bar.

In 1978, Sepot decided to once again open a restaurant at the location. During renovations, a large sign for Rudy's was uncovered on the side of the building. It read, "Rudy's Restaurant. Only Nite Spot in Fairfield. Visit Our Marine Room Catering to Private Parties, Weddings, Etc." The building was completely renovated, and Sepot changed the restaurant to Dogwood's. The menu explained the thinking behind the name:

When choosing a name for our restaurant we were looking for one that Fairfielders could identify with and our visitors could easily recognize. We also wanted our name to express the atmosphere and taste of our establishment. Dr. Isaac Bronson planted the first dogwood trees on Greenfield Hill over 180 years ago. Today there are over 2,000 dogwoods on the Hill. We think the dogwood tree with its simplicity, beauty and enduring strength express our idea perfectly.

The restaurant was family friendly with plenty of booths and large tables. The menu reflected the changing tastes of the times: lots of salads, sandwiches and burgers. Appetizers were simple: cucumbers marinated in red wine vinegar, stuffed mushrooms, fruit and sherbet cup. Of the entrées,

2070 Boston Post Road (Rte. 1)
in Historic Fairfield, Conn.
Telephone 255-2683

Named after Fairfield's famous trees, Dogwoods was a popular restaurant on the corner of Post Road and North Pine Creek Road. *Courtesy of Elly and Lorry Scott.*

OUR APPETIZERS

Fresh Garden Salad	.95
Cup of Soup	1.00
Cup of Onion Soup	1.25
Cup of Homemade Seafood Chowder	1.50
Quiche of the Day	1.50
Canneloni	1.50

(Our crepe filled with bits of chicken and veal spiced with herbs blended with ricotta cheese and topped with our chef's sauce.)

Fresh cucumbers marinated in red wine vinegar	.95
Stuffed Mushrooms	1.50
Breaded Mushrooms	1.25
Fruit and Sherbet Cup	1.50
Marinated Mushrooms	1.75
Shrimp Cocktail	3.25

OUR SALADS

Fresh Garden Salad	.95
Spinach—	2.75

Fresh spinach, with chunks of swiss, sliced egg and raw mushrooms.

Our Chef's Royal Salad—	3.50

Fresh lettuce, cucumbers, sliced egg, with roast beef, turkey, and ham, chunks of swiss and tomato — PHEW.

A Salad Lover's Special—	2.95

A choice of chicken, or tuna salad served on crisp lettuce with tomato slices and sliced egg.

Raw Veggie Plate & Dips	2.25

(A plate of the market's fresh veggies with dips and crackers)

The Thin Man—	3.25

Ham, roast beef and turkey with scoops of ham and chicken salad, lettuce and tomato.

Your choice of dressings. Roquefort .25¢ extra.

OUR SOUPS

A hearty bowl of soup. Served with our fresh garden salad and our homemade french bread.

Homemade French Onion Soup—	2.25

with a slice of toasted french bread and melted cheese.

Penfield's Old Fashioned Vegetable Soup—	1.95

assorted cut veggies with chunks of beef and chicken in a hearty beef broth.

Homemade Seafood Chowder—	2.50

with a touch of New England — A hearty chowder with clams, shrimp, the sea's catch, with assorted veggies, and finished with our chef's special touch.

Soup of the Day—	(Price as

Our chef's surprise — described by your waiter or waitress. (Price as announced.)

SOMETHING SPECIAL

Served with our fresh garden salad and our homemade french bread.

Our Chef's Special—
Luncheon and dinner entrees prepared by our chef. Described by your waiter or waitress. *(Price as announced.)*

Max's Delight—
Our freshly prepared fish of the day. Described by your waiter or waitress. *(Price as announced.)*

Mill Plain Cackle—	3.75/5.50

One or two boneless breasts of chicken covered with melted cheese and ham presented with rice pilaf.

Jumbo Pork Chops	4.75/6.75
A Colonial Feast—	4.50

A hearty order of chicken deep fried in our own special batter covered with fries.

Chicken Pot Pie—	3.95

Chunks of chicken or beef with assorted veggies baked in a light pie crust with our chef's special touch.

* Charlie's Overstuffed Cabbage	3.50/4.50

(Mondays only)

Tortellini	3.75

(Tuesdays only)
(Pasta Rings stuffed with chicken and cheese, smothered in a creamy cheese sauce)

OUR FILLERS

French Fries	.75
Onion Rings	.75
Cole Slaw	.75
Potato Salad	.75
Cottage Cheese	.85

OUR EXTRAS

Lettuce and Tomato	.20
Lettuce or Tomato	.15
Crisp Bacon	.25
Sauteed Onions	.20
Swiss Cheese	.20
American Cheese	.20

OUR BEVERAGES

Fruit Juices	.50
100% Colombian Coffee	.40
Tea	.40
Sanka	.40
Milk	.50
Soft Drinks	.50

OUR FROSTY BEERS

ON DRAUGHT

Michelob	.75
Miller	.75

BY THE BOTTLE

Budweiser	1.00
Miller Lite	1.00
Heineken	1.50
Molson Ale	1.50

Dogwoods restaurant, located in close proximity to the Fairfield train station, was a popular spot for commuters who wanted a light meal after working in New York City all day. *Courtesy of Elly and Lorry Scott.*

OUR SANDWICHES –

Served on white, rye, pumpernickel or hard roll and garnished appropriately.

Roast Beef	2.25
Baked Ham	2.25
Corned Beef	2.25
Pastrami	2.25
Turkey	2.25

*For $1.25 additional, enjoy ½ sandwich with any cup or bowl of soup or salad.

DOGWOODS' SPECIAL SANDWICH TREATS

The Reuben —	3.25
Thinly sliced corned beef, sauerkraut, swiss cheese and russian dressing served open faced.	
Dogwoods' Blossom —	2.95
Turkey, ham and roast beef with swiss cheese.	
Dogwoods' Delight —	2.95
Roast beef, corned beef and pastrami with swiss cheese and russian dressing.	
Kensie's Landing —	2.35
Roast beef and fresh spinach.	
Truby's Bell —	2.35
Roast beef and sliced raw onion.	
Barney's Delight —	2.25
Pastrami and melted swiss.	
Burr's Bag —	2.25
Pastrami and fried onions.	
Grasmere's Combo —	2.35
Pastrami, fried onions and melted swiss cheese.	
Harbor's Catch —	2.75
Tuna done our chef's way with bacon, lettuce and swiss served open faced.	
The Town Green Romp —	3.95
Choice sirloin slices with lettuce and tomato or sauteed onions served open faced on our homemade french bread.	
The Fairfield Club —	3.25
Slices of ham and turkey with crisp bacon, lettuce and tomato.	
The Lighthouse —	1.35
Grilled cheese and tomato.	
Greenfield's Special —	1.55
Grilled cheese, bacon and tomato.	

THE HOT ONES

Sasco's Special —	3.25
A jumbo sized hot open roast beef sandwich with our chef's special gravy and our fresh garden salad.	
Dawn's Special —	3.25
A jumbo sized hot turkey sandwich served open faced with our giblet gravy, and our fresh garden salad.	

OUR STEAKS

Due to a 45% cost increase in our steaks this week, we find it necessary to charge $1.00 additional to our menue price per steak. We regret this increase and assure you it is only done to maintain our high quality and standards.

Thank You

with sour cream and sliced bermuda onion.	
Barbequeburger —	2.50
marinated in our secret sauce — try it with cheese or bacon or both.	
Royalburger —	2.50
our burger crowned with a fried egg.	
Dogwoodburger Supreme —	2.75
our burger with lettuce, tomato, onion rings and fries — PHEW.	
Dieter's Burger —	2.50
our burger with a slice of tomato resting comfortably on a bed of lettuce — with a pineapple ring and cottage cheese.	

OUR STEAKS

Served with our fresh garden salad, baked potato, or french fries and our homemade french bread, grilled as you like.

The Sirloin —	6.75
A thick cut of top sirloin properly aged to bring out all the flavor.	
The Half-Cut —	5.25
A smaller cut of our sirloin for those whose eyes outdo their appetites.	
The New York Strip —	7.95
Cut from the bone, it's our tastiest steak.	
The Filet Mignon —	7.95
Our tenderest cut of beef.	
The Heartland —	5.75
Choice slices of london broil.	
The Creeker —	3.75
12 ounces of our fresh ground sirloin smothered with our special sauce.	

OUR STEWS

Served with our fresh garden salad and our homemade french bread.

The Hungarian Goulash —	3.75/4.75
Beef chunks sauteed in a paprika, wine and cream sauce seasoned with caraway seeds and onions served over hot buttered noodles.	
Chicken Cipotiene —	3.75/4.75
Chicken sauteed in butter and white wine with mushrooms, tomatoes and onions served with our special rice pilaf.	

Increasing beef prices in the 1980s caused many restaurants to raise their prices on steaks. Dogwoods was no exception. *Courtesy of Elly and Lorry Scott.*

Back when smoking was permitted in restaurants and an afternoon drink was acceptable, Dogwood's was a popular meeting spot for locals. Here, former chief of police Ron Sullivan, fire captain Charlie Phillips and Billy "the Barnacle" Gregorio enjoy some down time. *Courtesy of Joseph Sepot.*

there were a couple of nods to the town's Hungarian heritage: overstuffed cabbage and Hungarian goulash.

"People told me mixing steaks and sandwiches wouldn't work," said Sepot. "At the time, you either sold full dinners or you were a sandwich shop with no liquor license." But Sepot saw the potential of changing tastes in combination with the commuter lifestyle. At the time, commuters traveling back to Fairfield after working the day in Manhattan would often spend the hour-and-a-half trip in the bar car on the train. "Their wives would want dinner, but the commuters wouldn't want a full meal because they'd been drinking." Dogwoods filled that niche by offering both options.

A restaurant review in the *Fairpress* said Dogwoods was a pleasant addition to Fairfield dining. "As Fairfielders know best, the town has long cried for a restaurant of caliber and character," wrote Lou Gerber. "At last, one has arrived." The author enjoyed the soups, although he felt the feta cheese on the Mediterranean burger was simply "too strong to allow a burger's flavor to survive and the olive slices never had a chance."

Food tastes may have been changing, but at the bar, hard liquor was still in vogue. "The drinks were Scotch and water or vodka tonics," said Sepot. "Wine didn't come until the late '80s."

GROWING EMPIRES

With the huge success of Dogwoods, Sepot decided to open another restaurant on the other side of Fairfield. He took over the space that was the Continental and created Willowby's, the sister restaurant to Dogwoods. The menu explained:

> *Folklore has it that during the late 1700s, a man by the name of Ebeneezer Willowby, carrying little more than ale and good friendship, tended to and cared for the many willow trees that graced this area. Ebeneezer lived a long and merry life bringing entertainment and joy to many. We think his legend expresses our idea perfectly.*

The menu at Willowby's was similar to Dogwoods, with sandwiches and salads having names tied to local sites, such as the Rooster's River, Gypsy Springs and Stratfield's Combo. Unfortunately, the menu was a little too similar to the one at Dogwoods. "I killed my own self by having the same menu on the other side of town," said Sepot. "It wasn't my most brilliant move."

The building that housed Willowby's was changed from a restaurant to a business, while Dogwoods was taken over by Febbraio for Sidetracks. Less than a mile from the wildly popular Tommy's, Sidetracks was certainly a risk for Febbraio. "I didn't want to cannibalize Tommy's clientele," Febbraio said. Having seen the dilution of clientele between Dogwoods and Willowby's, Febbraio knew the risks. His vision for Sidetracks was an "American eatery, like a glorified diner." While Tommy's attracted the after-work, yuppie clientele, Sidetracks was more family- and blue-collar oriented with the occasional celebrity. "When I was growing up, we went to Sidetracks every couple months

226 Kings Highway East
Fairfield Ct. 06430
Telephone 576-9124

With the success of Dogwoods, owner Joseph Sepot decided to open a sister restaurant, Willowby's, on the opposite side of town. *Courtesy of Elly and Lorry Scott.*

OUR APPETIZERS

Fresh Garden Salad	1.25
Quiche of the Day	1.75
Canneloni	1.75
(Our crepe filled with bits of chicken and veal spiced with herbs blended with ricotta cheese and topped with our chef's sauce.)	
Antipasto	3.50
Clams Casino	3.50
Stuffed Mushrooms	2.50
Breaded Zucchini Sticks	1.75
(with our special dip)	
Marinated Mushrooms	1.75
Fresh Raw Veggie Plate	2.75
(A plate of the market's fresh veggies with dips and crackers.)	
Breaded Camembert	3.50
Cup of Vegetable Soup	1.50
Cup of Onion Soup	1.75
Cup of Seafood Chowder	1.95
Garlic Bread	1.25
Fruit and Cheese Board	2.75
Cup of our soup of the day	(Price as announced)

OUR SALADS

Spinach Salad —	1.95/2.95
Fresh spinach, with chunks of swiss, sliced egg and raw mushrooms.	
The Ringmaster —	3.50
Our Chef's Salad presented with fresh lettuce, cucumbers, sliced egg, in tandem with roast beef, turkey, and ham, chunks of swiss and tomato—WOW!!	
The Thin Person —	3.95
Ham, Roast Beef and Turkey escorted by scoops of ham and chicken salad on a bed of lettuce. Oh, yes—with slices of tomato.	
Monterey Peninsula —	4.95
A scoop of shrimp salad over fresh sprouts with swiss cheese, avocado slices, slices of tomato all residing on a bed of lettuce.	
Rooster's River —	3.95
Chicken salad nestled on a slice of pumpernickel with tomato, avocado slices and crisp bacon. Served with fresh fruit.	

OUR SOUPS

A Hearty Bowl of Soup. Our famous restaurant made soup served with our fresh garden salad and our special bread.

Penfield's Old Fashioned Vegetable Soup —	2.50
assorted cut veggies with chunks of beef and chicken in a hearty beef broth.	
French Onion Soup	2.75
Seafood Chowder —	2.95
with a touch of New England—A hearty chowder with clams, shrimp, the sea's catch, with assorted veggies, and finished with our chef's special touch.	
Soup of the Day —	(Price as announced)
Our chef's surprise—described by your waiter or waitress.	

OUR SANDWICHES

Served on white, rye, pumpernickel or hard roll and garnished appropriately.

Roast Beef —	2.55
(Cooked in our own ovens)	
Baked Ham	2.55
Corned Beef	2.55
Pastrami	2.55
Turkey	2.55
Tuna Fish	2.55
(on our special bread)	

*For $1.50 additional, enjoy ½ sandwich with any cup or bowl of soup or salad.

WILLOWBY'S SPECIAL SANDWICH TREATS

The Reuben —	3.55
Thinly sliced corned beef, our special sauerkraut, swiss cheese and Russian dressing served open faced.	
Willowby's Blossom —	3.25
Turkey, Ham and Roast Beef with swiss cheese.	
Willowby's Delight —	3.25
Roast Beef, Corned Beef, and Pastrami with swiss cheese and Russian dressing.	
The Willow's Lawn —	2.75
A mansion made with roast beef and fresh spinach.	
Villa's Volley —	2.75
Roast beef saturated with melted cheddar cheese.	
P.T.'s Delight —	2.65
Pastrami and melted swiss	
S.M.'s Dandy 1687 —	2.65
Pastrami and fried onions	
Stratfield's Combo —	2.75
Pastrami, fried onions, and melted swiss.	
Phipps' Beach —	3.25
Tuna done our chef's way with bacon and melted swiss served open faced	
The King's Highway —	4.55
Choice sirloin slices with lettuce and tomato or sauteed onions served open faced.	
Holland Hill's Club —	3.50
Slices of Ham and Turkey with crisp bacon, lettuce and tomato.	
The Pequonnuck —	1.50
Grilled cheese and tomato	
The Gypsy Springs —	1.75
Grilled cheese, bacon and tomato.	
Bostwick's Pop —	1.75
American cheese melted over sliced mushrooms and olives.	
The Bow Nosh —	1.75
Bagel with cream cheese and onion	
Knipper's Knapp —	2.95
Sliced tomato, onions, fresh mushroom slices, and spinach under a blanket of melted cheddar, served open faced on rye	

Many of the dishes at Willowby's were named after Fairfield sites, such as the King's Highway and Rooster's River. *Courtesy of Elly and Lorry Scott.*

GATE 1
SIDECAR APPETIZERS

CHICKEN FINGERS 7.95
With honey mustard and barbecue dips, or Buffalo style!

WESTERN STYLE FILET TIPS 8.95
Pan-seared and served with jalapeno mayonnaise

BAKED BRIE 7.95
Garnished with French bread and seasonal fruit

FRIED MOZZARELLA STICKS 5.95
Golden brown, with marinara sauce on the side

FRIED CALAMARI & DIPPING SAUCES 7.95

POTATO SKINS 6.95
With melted cheddar and choice of bacon or broccoli toppings

CHICKEN QUESADILLA 7.95
With grilled red onions, scallions, black beans & pineapple salsa

SIDETRACKS NACHOS 11.95/10.95
Our legendary platter, jumbo or regular size

BUFFALO WINGS 7.95
Spicy jumbo wings, served with celery & creamy gorgonzola dip

FORK AND KNIFE PIZZA 8.95
Thin crust tortilla topped with spicy ground beef or grilled chicken topped with Monterey Jack, diced tomatoes, black olives

GATE 2
SOUP AND SALAD DINER

TOMMY'S FAMOUS BISQUE 4.95/5.95
Borrowed from our older brother...

FRENCH ONION SOUP 4.95
Topped with melted Finlandia cheese

SPICY BEEF CHILI 5.95
With melted cheddar, sour cream & tortilla chips

CHUDDY'S SALAD 7.95
Tuna or curried chicken, served with creamy dill dressing on the side

GRAND CENTRAL CHICKEN SALAD 8.95
Grilled strips served with honey dill dressing

SHRIMP OR CHICKEN CAESAR 11.95/9.95
With traditional tangy dressing

SIDETRACKS SALAD 8.95
Curried diced chicken, tomatoes, artichokes, on a slice of pineapple with walnut dressing

CHINATOWN CHICKEN SALAD 8.95
Over mixed greens & tossed with soba noodles, and sesame-ginger dressing

GLAZED ATLANTIC SALMON SALAD 10.95
Over mixed greens with seasonal citrus fruit, tossed with grapefruit-sesame vinaigrette

MEDDITERANEAN 9.95
Artichoke hearts, roasted peppers and grilled eggplant tossed with mixed greens and balsamic vinaigrette (Add grilled chicken for 3.95)

Sidetracks became known for its huge platters of nachos, which came with chili, refried beans, jalapeño peppers and sour cream. *Courtesy of Elly and Lorry Scott.*

as a casual-but-nice treat," said Megan Stanish. "One time, my mom became very still. When she finally spoke, she whispered to us that Jason Robards was sitting at the next table. I looked over my shoulder, and sure enough, there he was."

The bar area was always busy and was maintained by David "Buddy" Berger. "Everyone who came in knew Buddy," said Febbraio. With the dawn of the '80s came a changing bar scene. The hard liquor and brown spirits drinks of the '70s were being replaced by sweet blender drinks. At Sidetracks, one of the most popular beverages was a frozen mudslide.

Febbraio capitalized on the railroad theme and went to auctions in Hershey, Pennsylvania, to purchase artifacts to decorate the restaurant. There were railroad signs and stop lights throughout the restaurant, but the most notable feature was a train that circled the upstairs and whistled as it chugged by. More than a few parents were known to enjoy dinner while their kids stayed upstairs staring at the train.

"I used to live in the townhouses across the street from Sidetracks," said Christine Jeffrey. "The smell of their teriyaki steak grilling used to drive me to distraction. Needless to say we ate there often. I loved their curried

Above: Sidetracks was a family-friendly restaurant and offered a children's menu. *Courtesy of Elly and Lorry Scott.*

Right: The menu at Sidetracks offered a little bit of everything. *Courtesy of Elly and Lorry Scott.*

Gate 3
Trans-Milano Trolley

Chicken Pasta Pie 15.95
Smoked chicken tossed with penne pasta, mushrooms, roasted red peppers and scallions in a light Alfredo sauce and topped with Mozzarella or marinara sauce.

Big Bowl Chicken n' Sausage Pasta 15.95
Chunks of chicken breast and sweet Italian sausage with tomatoes, garlic & white wine-butter sauce, served over house-made rigatoni in a big bowl!

Chicken Marsala 15.95
Pan-seared chicken breast with wild mushrooms, pignoli nuts, diced prosciuto and marsala wine

Chicken Neopolitan 15.95
Sauteed chicken breast with mushrooms, marinara sauce, and cherry peppers over housemade rigatoni

Chicken Parmigiana 15.95
With a side of house-made penne pasta

Three Cheese Ravioli 14.95
Made with ricotta, parmesan and fontinella cheeses

Gate 4
Mexicali Grande Platters

Arizona Chicken Taco Salad 13.95
A bounteous meal, with tomatoes, sour cream, guacamole, refried beans and melted cheeses on a bed of rice and mixed greens in a crispy taco shell bowl.

Fajita in a Pita 8.95
Flank steak, chicken or veggie, served with onions, peppers & Monterey Jack cheese

Chicken Ranchero 15.95
Sautéed chicken with Bermuda onions, peppers, scallions and salsa, and melted Monterey Jack cheese over rice

Steak or Chicken Fajitas 15.95
With refried beans, sour cream, pico de gallo, guacamole, peppers, onions and nacho cheese

Chimichanga 14.95
Choice of chicken or beef! With aged Monterey Jack cheese, sour cream, pico de gallo, guacamole. Rice and refried beans on the side

Sidings...Handful or Basket of Fries $1.00/$2.50 ...

Please note...We a

GATE 5
SANDWICH JUNCTION

PHILADELPHIA TERMINAL 8.95
Sliced sirloin or chicken, sautéed onions &
American cheese
METRO CLUB CAR 7.95
Turkey breast, bacon, lettuce, tomato & mayon-
naise, on toast
BARBECUED PORK 7.95
Slow-cooked 'n tender barbecue pork loin piled high
on a Portuguese roll
SANTE FE CHICKEN 8.95
Marinated boneless breast with melted Monterey Jack
cheese, bacon, lettuce & tomato, plus guacamole
CHICKEN REUBEN 8.95
Seedless rye, flat-grilled with American cheese,
tomato, avocado, cole slaw and honey mustard
PASTRAMI STEAMER 8.95
Fresh steamed pastrami with Swiss cheese, cole
slaw and pickle
SAUTÉED CHICKEN CUTLET 8.95
With fresh mozzarella, roasted peppers, lettuce, tomato
and pesto mayonnaise.

(All Sandwiches served with pasta salad, pickle)

Gate 6
Boxcar Burgers

Basic Railburger (10 oz.) 6.95
(Ask for lettuce, tomato, mayo, onions!)
Bacon Cheeseburger 7.95
Mushroomburger 7.95
Sidetracksburger 7.95
(Gorgonzola cheese, Bermuda onions, lettuce & tomato)
Californiaburger 7.95
(Monterey Jack, guacamole, lettuce & tomato)
Turkeyburger! 6.95
(Housemade, with Cranberry-mayo, lettuce & tomato)

Onion Rings $3.50 ... Tub of Guacamole $0.95

atically charge a 17.5% gratuity for parti

Sandwiches and burgers were popular with
commuters who spent the previous two hours in the
bar car of the train. *Courtesy of Elly and Lorry Scott.*

chicken salad that was served in half a pineapple. I still make mine using their secret ingredient." What was the secret ingredient? A drizzle of maple syrup.

Febbraio described the menu as a combination and variation of different menus. "We had great burgers," he said. "A favorite was the Fajita in a Pita. It was a fun, family eatery that was priced for value."

But of all the things that Sidetracks had going for it, nothing compared to the nachos. Oh, the nachos. They were the stuff legends were made of. Diners could order a half or a full order, and a mountain of cheese-covered chips would arrive on a hot iron plate. On the side would be ramekins of refried beans, pico de gallo, guacamole and salsa. "People all over the country talked about them," said Febbraio. So what made them so special? "The cheese," said Febbraio. "We had it flown in from a small little company in New Mexico. We UPS-ed it in two times a week." The cheese was a combination of Monterey Jack, yellow cheddar and white cheddar. "We were going through so much of it we talked Cisco [the food company] into carrying it."

In addition to the special cheese, the chips were also unique. They were fried in the restaurant and the cheese was melted in between each layer of chips, rather than just dumped on the top.

THE BEST THINGS COME IN SMALL PACKAGES

Less than a half mile away from Sidetracks, the tiny building that once housed Kowalsky's—and then briefly a restaurant called Ann's Place—was about to undergo a dramatic makeover. Marty Levine was studying the restaurant business in school. He was also observing how local restaurants, like the Player's Tavern and Mario's in Westport, were operating. "It looked like a good business," he said. "I liked music; I liked the atmosphere."

The bar scene took a turn in the '80s with the rising popularity of frozen drinks. Breakaway was known for its creative frozen "stimulators." *Courtesy of Alison Healy.*

Ched
Swiss } chuses
amer } avail.

BREAKAWAY

SERVING EVERYDAY 11:30 A.M. TO 10:00 P.M.
FRIDAY AND SATURDAY TO 11:00 P.M.

SENSATIONS ▐▐▐▐▐▐▐▐▐▐▐▐▐▐▐▐▐▐▐▐▐▐▐▐▐

An array of different and delicious daily specials. All specials are chosen for quality, freshness, and seasonal availability. Absolutely outstanding!

Try our special drinks and homemade desserts.

SPECTACULARS ▐▐▐▐▐▐▐▐▐▐▐▐▐▐▐▐▐▐▐▐▐▐

BROILED CHICKEN/with steak fries. *Br. chix*. . . 6.95
BARBEQUE CHICKEN/with steak fries. *BB @chix*. 7.25
BARBEQUE BABYBACK RIBS/with steak fries
and cole slaw. . . . *Ribs* 10.50
BARBEQUE COMBO — CHICKEN AND RIBS/with
steak fries and cole slaw. . . *Combo* 10.95
N.Y. STRIP STEAK . . . . . . *N.Y.* 12.95

BEEFERS ▐▐▐▐▐▐▐▐▐▐▐▐▐▐▐▐▐▐▐▐▐▐▐▐▐▐▐▐

BOUNTIFUL BURGERS OF CHOPPED SIRLOIN, SERVED
WITH LETTUCE, TOMATO AND STEAK FRIES ON A
HARD ROLL
BURGER/just a plain burger burger. *Pl. burg*. 4.50
SLIMMER/served bunless with cottage cheese
and fruit garnish. . *Slimmer* 4.75
CHARMER/american and swiss. . *Charmer*. 4.75
MADNESS/herbs and sauteed *mad - mad/sw*
mushrooms. . . . . . 4.50 with cheese 4.95
CLASSY/canadian bacon and cheddar *Classy* 4.95
CHILIBURGER/chili topped with
melted cheddar . . . *Chili burg* 5.25

Just barely a hole in the wall, Breakaway was a popular place for a specialty burger. *Courtesy of Alison Healy.*

Levine spent some time in Denver, Colorado, but decided to return to Fairfield. "On the way back, I stopped at a gas station right across from what was then called Ann's Place. I had no idea this was going to be my destiny," he said.

The tiny building became available in 1980, and twenty-four-year-old Levine saw his opportunity to create a one-of-a-kind "edgy" restaurant. He bought it and named the restaurant Breakaway. "We painted it a lot of colors," he said. There were tropical pinks, peaches and teals. "At first I thought it was a mistake," he said. The bar was small, and the tables were packed in. Breakaway was not a place for quiet, personal conversation. But it was the place for good food and friendly banter. "The clientele was totally mixed, across the board," said Levine. There were commuters in suits, ladies who lunched and blue-collar workers just getting off their shifts. "Reservations aren't accepted," an article from 1987 explained.[133] "It would screw up the melting-pot quality. Those folks with alligators on their polo shirts might elbow out the Harley contingent, and everyone would wonder how things turned sour."

The menu consisted mostly of omelets, salads, sandwiches and burgers. One hot seller was the Waldorf chicken salad. Another was the Royal Gorge, a baguette cut on the bias with turkey, Canadian bacon, Russian dressing, tomatoes and melted cheese.

"This was the time when people drank at lunch," said Levine. "They'd have two or three martinis. Now, at the most, people have a glass of wine." But that wasn't the only difference.

"Every single table had an ashtray on it," said Levine. "At night, you could see this wafting, billowing smoke in the lights." Breakaway was continually packed and became known for its frozen drinks. There were the usual daiquiris and piña coladas, but also drinks like the Macaroon (amaretto, almond paste, coconut milk and cream) and the Strawberry Banana Split (banana liqueur, Myer's rum, strawberries, bananas and cream). According to local legend, the bartender hated making the blender drinks. When it got to be too much, he'd instruct the waitresses to tell the diners that the blender was broken.

Levine operated Breakaway for six and a half years. In 1986, he bought the property, and in 1987, he sold the business. It became Rory's. After a few more years, the building needed major work. "As they say in the business, the building was fully depreciated," said Levine. Rory's closed in 2007. Demolition began and a new building—the same size as the tiny Breakaway—was built. In 2009, Levine opened Martel, a French-inspired bistro.

SATISFYING FAIRFIELD'S SWEET TOOTH

Cakes and Pies

An old black-and-white photograph dated 1909 depicts three bakers in their white aprons standing outside of a store front. With them are three children, a woman and a dog. It's a scene right out of the *Our Gang* "Roamin' Holiday" episode. (You can almost imagine the boys sitting on the steps eating the pies and cakes they swindled from Mrs. Jenks.) This was Hall's Home Made Bakery, presumably one of the town's first bakeries. The picture was taken at the original store, which was located on the Post Road, where the children's library would stand nearly fifty years later.

Little is now known of the bakery or the Hall family, but they were a definite presence in town at the time. In the summer of 1911, a fireman's fair was held. The newspaper reported, "John Dunleavy was the lucky holder of the ticket which won the immense cake given by John Hall of the Hall Bakery Company."[134]

Business must have been good because in 1913 it was reported, "The value of auto over horse has found favor with Dominic Mercurio, the local fruit man, and also with Hall, the baker. Both now have business cars."[135]

Life wasn't entirely rosy, though, as illness struck the family. The paper reported, "Laura Hall, daughter of Mr. Hall of the Home Made Bakery,

Opposite, top: One of the town's first bakeries, Hall's stood from 1909 to 1925 on the spot where the children's library would later be built. *Left to right*: Laura Hall, John Hall, an employee, Jack Dietrich, Eugenie Hall, Antoinette Hall and Anna Bock. *Courtesy of the Fairfield Museum and History Center.*

In 1925, Hall's Home Made Bakery moved to the corner of Reef and Post Roads, next to Clampett's. *Courtesy of the Fairfield Museum and History Center.*

who has been ill for some time with scarlet fever, is rapidly recovering and the house will soon be out of quarantine." One can only imagine that the bakery receipts went down for a bit after that announcement.[136]

In 1925, the bakery was torn down, and the business was moved to the corner of Reef and Post Roads, next to Clampett's Drug Store.

But Hall's wasn't the only game in town. On the corner of the Post Road and Beaumont Street on the first floor of a brick building was Devore's, which was opened in 1921 by Celia and Michael Devore.

THE AFTER-CHURCH CROWD

Sunday mornings in Fairfield meant one thing for most children: church. But if you were lucky enough, it also meant donuts.

Sure, there were glossy loaves of rye bread (with or without seeds), chewy salt sticks, crumb cake dusted with powdered sugar, cookies of all kinds and layer cakes with thick buttercream frosting. But it was the donuts that attracted young and old alike. When you entered, bells would jingle against the front door signaling the arrival of a customer. To the left was the donut machine.

"From 1948 until the mid-1950s, the donut machine was in the front window and alongside it was a spanking white paper bag into which was placed any donut that fell to the floor by mistake. After school, I'd run down to Devore's with a friend or two and hope the bag was full of discards which were happily given to us by the owner/operator," wrote Edward McLaughlin. "That would not happen today with current health regulations but back then it was 'heaven' to receive warm donuts for free."[137]

In the late 1920s, donuts were twenty-five cents a dozen. And, oh, what donuts they were. There were light as air glazed donuts; soft powdered sugar donuts; dense cinnamon-sugar donuts; and fat, overstuffed jelly donuts. It was the promise of one of these coveted donuts that got the local children through Sunday Mass without squirming.

"My family went to Mass every Sunday morning at St. Anthony's," said Rosemarie Corr. The church was located just a few blocks away from the bakery. "The aroma of baking bread and fresh donuts greeted us as we walked out of church. My father would take us there and while the ladies sliced the rye bread for him, one of the other ladies would let us each pick out a cookie."[138]

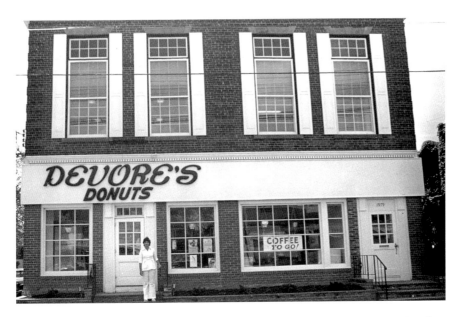

First opened in the 1920s, Devore's was the place to go for fresh baked goods after church on Sundays. *Courtesy of the Fairfield Museum and History Center.*

Carol Black worked behind the counter of Devore's. "I remember working Sunday mornings from seven to one. There was a mad crush for about thirty minutes after the Masses got out. I still love cheese Danish to this day. I haven't found any that are as good as Devore's."[139]

One of the mainstays of Devore's was Nora O'Hara. Her granddaughter, Linda Malkin, remembers those days. She said:

> *My grandmother Nora O'Hara worked there. I remember visiting Gram who took us to see the bakers in the back. I loved watching the bread slicer. My favorite when I was younger were the powdered or cinnamon jelly donuts. Later, were the huge chocolate chip cookies and the plain cinnamon donuts. We got all our birthday and other celebration cakes there. Prune, apple and raspberry mini-Danish were also yummy. Gram's favorite was probably the pound cake to have with her tea.*
>
> *The bakery smelled like sugar and/or bread baking when you walked in the door. The glass case was straight ahead and the bread slicer was over to the left against the wall near the swinging door that went to the back where the magic happened. My grandmother worked there until she was in her eighties. She lived in the grey house that was just behind Devore's. They used to make her take the money bag home at night. How dangerous would*

that be these days? We used to ride our bikes from Ludlowe [the high school] *to visit Gram at the bakery after high school. There was always a tasty treat awaiting us.* [140]

Devore's provided afterschool jobs for many local kids. Jonathan Chernes recalls his memories:

Every Sunday morning, my grandfather would come home with the Sunday papers and bags from Devore's—hard rolls, jelly donuts and a big chocolate chip cookie for me. I'd gorge myself while reading the comics. Then, when I was in the fourth grade, I got a "job" there sweeping up and cleaning the windows. I was paid in donuts. I don't remember how long it lasted, but I loved it. [141]

While many people associate Devore's with Sundays, others remember the bakery from the town's annual Memorial Day parade, an event beloved by citizens of all ages.

"The Memorial Day parade used to begin way down there on the side street next to Devore's," said Dolores Abbott. "Waiting to assemble with my fellow Girl Scouts to get into parade formation, I would always have a jelly donut. I'm not sure who bought it. My father would be nearby, assembled with the Father Coleman Knights of Columbus, so maybe the Knights in their ostrich feather hats and tuxedos would spring for the donuts. I continue to associate jelly donuts with Memorial Day." [142] Meanwhile, Jessie Murphy remembers being warned not to eat any donuts before the parade for fear that powdered sugar would get all over their uniforms. [143]

SWEETS FOR SERVICEMEN

The bakery was passed down through three generations of the Devore family before it was sold in 1985 to Bob and Judy Oracheff. [144] They continued making the famous donuts and breads that the bakery was known for and were awarded a contract to provide doughnuts and baked goods to eight thousand navy personnel stationed at the naval submarine base in Groton, Connecticut. On any given day, Devore's would be pumping out 100 to 120 dozen doughnuts for the servicemen. Their favorites were glazed doughnuts, followed closely by chocolate-glazed cake doughnuts. The bakery hired two additional bakers and a full-time driver to accommodate the naval base. After several years, Bob and Judy handed the business over to their son, Mike Oracheff, and his wife, Dawn. They expanded the business by wholesaling the baked goods to local food stores, delis and gas stations.

Rumors started to fly, though, in 1998 when local newspapers reported that the bakery had filed for bankruptcy. The dispute concerned another business, but the bakery was used as collateral.[145] They managed to pull through, though, and the ovens kept churning out the baked goods. In 2005, Oracheff added a delicatessen within the bakery and things seemed to be status quo.[146]

It came as a huge surprise, then, in 2006 when the bakery suddenly shut its doors. Citing a combination of rising costs, exorbitant rent, competition from national chains and a shortage of parking spaces, Oracheff decided it was time to close. "We couldn't keep the shop moving," he said in an article printed in the *Connecticut Post*. "It's just too much for a small-business owner. I think a lot of mom-and-pop shops are done."[147]

With the bakery gone, residents mourned the loss of freshly made doughnuts and giant chocolate chip cookies. And then, seemingly out of the blue, a tiny shop on the opposite side of town opened in 2010. The sign read, "The Original Devore Doughnut Shop." It was true. Michael Oracheff had decided to give the doughnuts another shot, albeit in a smaller location on Brooklawn Avenue on the Fairfield/Bridgeport line. Inventory was limited due to the size of the store, but doughnuts, cookies and pastries were highlights.[148] Sadly, the shop closed in 2012.

Devore's Irish Soda Bread[149]

Ingredients for dough:
½ cup sugar
½ cup powdered milk
Pinch salt
5 cups all-purpose flour
2½ cups cake flour
⅓ cup baking powder
½ cup shortening

1. Place all the above ingredients in a mixing bowl and mix for 5 minutes with bread hook or paddle.

Remainder of ingredients:
1 cup eggs
3 cups water
⅓ cup Caraway seeds (optional)
1¼ cups raisins (optional)

2. Add the eggs and water and mix for 5 minutes. The dough will be very sticky.
3. Divide this dough into three portions using flour to round and expedite handling. It's sticky! Don't worry about flour ruining your mix.
4. Set each floured ball on a baking sheet lined with parchment paper and sprinkle a little flour on top.
5. Cut a 4-inch X across the top
6. Bake at 400 degrees for 50–55 minutes until golden brown. To check, push lightly on the top center of the bread. If firm, bread is done.
7. Remove from oven and place on wire racks to cool.

FAIRFIELD'S PIECE OF THE PIE

With its yellow and brown décor; big, shiny globe light bulbs; and glass display cases, the Pie Plate restaurant was the place to get dessert from the early 1970s through the early 1990s. "I loved the pre–Mork and Mindy décor—rainbows, '70s san serif fonts. It was such a happy place," said Elizabeth Van De Bogart.[150]

Owner Art Green was a former baker for Oronoque Orchards, a bakery in Shelton, Connecticut. He decided to open his own chain of Connecticut-based pie-themed restaurants.[151] The original storefront was in Waterbury, and in 1972, he opened the Fairfield location. Set in a strip mall near "the circle," the Pie Plate was more than just pies. The large menu offered diners everything from soup and sandwiches to full meals. But of course, it was the pie that attracted people.

"We were always busy," said Beth Herde, a waitress at the Pie Plate from 1977 to 1980. "I can remember times when the line was out the door."[152] Green said that regulars would come in and sit in the same seat, look at the menu and order the same thing they always did.

Wearing a uniform of white pants and a white turtleneck shirt with a red smock, Herde would wait on customers who would have a hard time choosing from the dozens of varieties of pies. On the regular menu, there was apple, of course, and other fruit pies such as blueberry, peach, strawberry rhubarb, apricot, pineapple and cherry. For a short time in the summer, fresh strawberry pies were available. The strawberries, some as big as a fist, would come in crates, and the staff would work extra hours hulling them. Droves of people would come out for the fresh strawberry pie. Then there were the cream and custard pies: banana, banana fudge, chocolate, black bottom, pineapple, coconut, apple, blueberry and cherry. Then there were the "prize

All pies from the Pie Plate—whether they were chocolate cream, apple or fresh strawberry—came in the iconic tin dish. *Courtesy of Dolores Abbott and Nick Gamma.*

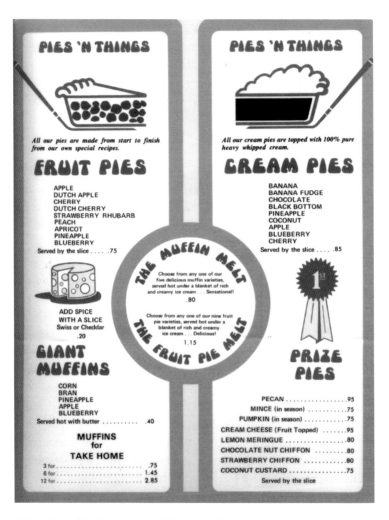

PIES 'N THINGS

All our pies are made from start to finish from our own special recipes.

FRUIT PIES

APPLE
DUTCH APPLE
CHERRY
DUTCH CHERRY
STRAWBERRY RHUBARB
PEACH
APRICOT
PINEAPPLE
BLUEBERRY
Served by the slice 75

ADD SPICE
WITH A SLICE
Swiss or Cheddar
.20

GIANT MUFFINS

CORN
BRAN
PINEAPPLE
APPLE
BLUEBERRY
Served hot with butter 40

MUFFINS
for
TAKE HOME
3 for 75
6 for 1.45
12 for 2.85

PIES 'N THINGS

All our cream pies are topped with 100% pure heavy whipped cream.

CREAM PIES

BANANA
BANANA FUDGE
CHOCOLATE
BLACK BOTTOM
PINEAPPLE
COCONUT
APPLE
BLUEBERRY
CHERRY
Served by the slice 85

THE MUFFIN MELT
Choose from any one of our five delicious muffin varieties, served hot under a blanket of rich and creamy ice cream . . . Sensational!
.80

THE FRUIT PIE MELT
Choose from any one of our nine fruit pie varieties, served hot under a blanket of rich and creamy ice cream . . . Delicious!
1.15

PRIZE PIES

PECAN 95
MINCE (in season) 75
PUMPKIN (in season) 75
CREAM CHEESE (Fruit Topped) 95
LEMON MERINGUE 80
CHOCOLATE NUT CHIFFON 80
STRAWBERRY CHIFFON 80
COCONUT CUSTARD 75
Served by the slice

Although the Pie Plate served a full menu, pies were the reason people came. Swiss or cheddar cheese could be added to any slice of pie for an additional twenty cents. *Courtesy of Sue Steele.*

pies"—pecan, mince, pumpkin, cream cheese with fruit, lemon meringue, chocolate nut chiffon, strawberry chiffon and coconut custard. Pie was served by the slice, and for an extra twenty cents, you could have your pie in true New England style and add a slice of Swiss or cheddar cheese. "People really liked the Dutch apple pie," said Herde. "The other waitresses and I used to pick the crumbs off the top and eat them when we walked by."

And at the end of the evening, the waitstaff would get to take home any pies that had been cut into.

Of course, there were savory pies, too: quiche Lorraine, chicken pot pie, turkey pot pie and seafood pot pie. The menu also included burgers, sandwiches and salads. If you were watching your waistline, you could order from the "Thin's In" section: a burger or sliced turkey on a bed of lettuce with tomato wedges, cottage cheese and egg slices. But really, if you were on a diet, chances were you wouldn't be at the Pie Plate.

One former customer recalled:

> *My parents always felt like if we had dinner there first, it was okay to have some pie. So we ate dinner there a lot. Mumbo Gumbo soup with that awesome mini-loaf of warm bread for a light supper. Chicken pot pies were awesome and Dad usually had a Black Russian hamburger. It was a grilled burger, fried onions, Swiss cheese and Russian dressing, on pumpernickel bread, and then grilled the entire sandwich like a Reuben or a grilled cheese. We also went there frequently for coffee and pie. Mom and Dad used to bring those muffins to me when I was at college.*

The muffins were almost as legendary as the pie. The muffins—corn, bran, pineapple, apple, blueberry and chocolate chip—were giant, rectangular and served hot, dripping with butter. Or, if you were feeling particularly decadent, there was the Muffin Melt: a hot muffin with a scoop of ice cream.

Patricia Nichols still laughs about one memorable visit to the Pie Plate. She and her husband went for breakfast. "We ordered and waited forever to get our food. That was very unusual. All of a sudden a man burst out of the kitchen and ran out the door. Our waitress gingerly came over and told us the cook just quit and there would be no breakfast."[153]

Needless to say, around Thanksgiving and Christmas, there would be line out the door and down the sidewalk as people waited to get their holiday pies.

The Pie Plate closed in June 1996 because there were plans to demolish the building in order to make room for a new Stop & Shop. That November, the Pie Plate did reopen the week before Thanksgiving in order to accommodate holiday pie requests. In 1997, Art Green opened "Art Green Coffee & Tea Company" on Black Rock Turnpike, which only remained in business for a short time.[154]

ᎩOU SCREAM, Ꮙ SCREAM...

What would a coastal town be without an ice cream shop or two? Fairfield, with its long stretch of beaches and large population of children, is the perfect setting for an old-fashioned ice cream parlor. Over the years, ice cream shops have come and gone, but there has always been at least one spot where you could get a cone on a hot summer day.

Buddy's Store, located on Reef Road near Penfield Beach, first opened in 1933. In the summers, customers would come in and out of the store all day, looking for a sandwich or a cup of coffee. But those in the know would head to the back of the store where nine red stools lined up along a red counter. While jazz records played, kids and teens would gather. Behind the counter, many canisters and pumps lined the wall, ready to disperse syrups and flavorings for sundaes, frappés and ice cream sodas.[155] It was the quintessential seaside soda fountain.

But ice cream didn't just have a sweet side. Who knew that it would be a source of controversy? In 1895, there was talk of eliminating the sale of ice cream on Sundays in Fairfield. Why? To keep out the bad element, of course. With the recent launch of the trolley, "Southport residents complained that too many Bridgeporters came to town every Sunday; they were not as respectful of the Sabbath as Southporters thought they ought to be." The newspaper of the time, the *Southport Chronicle*, reported that townspeople were "in favor of doing something to restrict the people who came to Southport and behave in an unseemly manner."[156] One idea that was bandied about was to ban the sale of ice cream in an effort to make the trip to Southport less desirable. Presumably they were headed to Bulkley's Ice Cream Store on Main Street. Needless to say, that idea didn't get very far.

Over the years, there were the usual chain ice cream shops that came and went. There was Baskin Robbins, which had a couple of different locations, and Carvel, next to McDonald's in "the circle," where one could get Flying Saucers or a Fudgie the Whale ice cream cake.

TWENTY-EIGHT FLAVORS

In November 1956, a Howard Johnson's restaurant opened on the Post Road under the management of Irving Carter. With its iconic orange roof and turquoise steeple, the restaurant was an instant hit among Fairfield residents. It was an affordable option for families, and the menu offered something for everyone. And with the impending construction of the Fairfield section of I-95, the restaurant offered an easy on/ easy off location for travelers. But perhaps its biggest draw was the ice cream. HoJo's was famous for its "28 flavors of ice cream." It offered the usual flavors—chocolate, vanilla and strawberry—but also more exotic flavors like burgundy cherry, Swiss chocolate almond and bisque tortoni. Popular favorites were peppermint stick and orange-pineapple, and classics like maple walnut, pistachio and butter pecan were big sellers.

Brenda Wilson practically grew up at the Fairfield

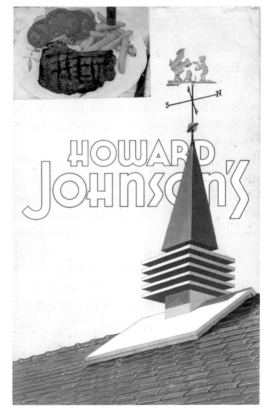

With its iconic orange roof, Howard Johnson's was a welcome site for hungry travelers. *Courtesy of Sue Steele.*

ice cream and sundaes

Howard Johnson's Ice Cream
Choice of Flavors 25

Howard Johnson's Sherbet
Orange, Raspberry, or Lime 25

THESE DELICIOUS SUNDAES INCLUDE
Whipped Cream or Marshmallow
and Choice of
Walnuts, Pecans

Howard Johnson's	Blueberry	.60
Famous Chocolate .50	Crushed Pineapple	.60
Vanilla Maple 50	Coffee Fudge	.60
Maple Nut 60	Hot Butterscotch	.60
Hot Fudge 60	Chocolate	
Maple Fudge 60	Marshmallow . .	.60
Fresh Sliced	Maraschino	
Strawberry . . . -.60	Cherry	.60

Howard Johnson's Celebrated
STRAWBERRY ICE CREAM SHORTCAKE
Vanilla Ice Cream on Golden Sponge
Cake with Luscious Red Strawberries,
topped with Whipped Cream . . . . . . **75¢**

BANANA ROYAL 75
On a BANANA, a scoop of VANILLA ICE CREAM
covered with Crushed Pineapple, a scoop of STRAW-
BERRY ICE CREAM covered with Strawberry Fruit,
Whipped Cream and topped with Nuts and a Cherry.

TASTY-TESTER 60
Four Scoops of our Delicious Ice Cream
Your Choice of Flavors

sodas and milk drinks

Ice Cream Sodas, All Flavors 45

Milk Shakes (All Flavors) 35

Floats (All Flavors) 45

Malted Milk (All Flavors) 40

Frappes (All Flavors) 45

Double-Thick Shake 40
(Vanilla, Chocolate, Coffee) "The DRINK You EAT With a Spoon"

Egg Shake (All Flavors) 45

Egg Malted Milk (All Flavors) 45

beverages

Cup of Coffee 15   Pot of Tea 15
Howard Johnson's Orange Drink   .15
Milk 15   Root Beer 15
Orange Freeze 35   Hot Chocolate 20

63 NE 8

Howard Johnson's. "My mother Natalie Petro worked there for twenty years," she said. "My mother was like a fixture there. Everybody knew and loved Natalie." In fact, her whole family worked there at different times. "That was our first job when we became old enough," said Wilson. "It was like family there."[157]

So much so that Wilson said all of her Thanksgiving memories were from Howard Johnson's. The restaurant was open 364 days a year; it closed only on Christmas. "Since my mother worked Thanksgiving, we all got to go have Thanksgiving dinner with her for free," said Wilson. She recalled that it was always busy for the holiday. "I remember they served everything from soup and nuts to dessert. It was always a big deal."

Wilson worked there as a waitress, donning her brown polyester uniform and white nurse's shoes. "It was a good, but tiring, job. You were on your feet most of the time," she said. "Back in those days, everybody

No meal at Howard Johnson's was complete without one of their famous sundaes. *Courtesy of Sue Steele.*

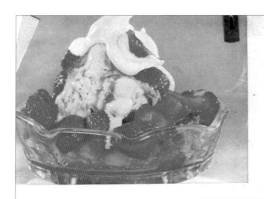

HOWARD JOHNSON'S
Strawberry Ice Cream Shortcake

Vanilla Ice Cream on Golden
Sponge Cake with Luscious Red
Strawberries topped with
Whipped Cream

75c

HOWARD JOHNSON'S
ice creams

Banana
Bisque Tortoni
Black Raspberry
Burgundy Cherry
Butter Pecan
Butter Crunch
Caramel Fudge
Cherry Vanilla
Chocolate
Chocolate Chip
Coffee
Coconut
Fudge Ripple
Lemon
Maple Walnut
Mocha Chip
Mint Chocolate Chip
Mocha Walnut
Peach
Peppermint Stick
Pineapple
Pistachio
Strawberry
Swiss Almond
Vanilla

sherbets

Lemon Lime
Orange Raspberry

sodas and milk drinks

Ice Cream Sodas	.45
Milk Shakes (All Flavors)	.35
Floats (All Flavors)	.45
Malted Milk (All Flavors) . . .	.40
Double-Thick Shake	.40
(Vanilla, Chocolate, Coffee)	
"The DRINK You EAT With a Spoon"	
Root Beer or Coca-Cola	.15
With Ice Cream	.30

specials

BANANA ROYAL 75
On a banana, a scoop of vanilla
ice cream covered with crushed
pineapple, a scoop of strawberry ice cream covered with
strawberry fruit, whipped cream
and topped with nuts and a cherry

BLUEBERRY SUNDAE 50
Vanilla ice cream, topped with
blueberry sauce and whipped
cream

HOWARD JOHNSON'S
Apple Pie

With Our Own
Vanilla Ice Cream
40c

Decisions, decisions. No doubt, it was a tough choice to choose between the strawberry ice cream shortcake and the apple pie à la mode at Howard Johnson's. *Courtesy of Sue Steele.*

Play

HOWARD JOHNSON'S
ICE CREAM GAME

Check the popular flavors as you try them

Vanilla	☐	Buttercrunch	☐	
Chocolate	☐	Pistachio	☐	
Strawberry	☐	Maple Walnut	☐	
Coffee	☐	Banana	☐	
Butter Pecan	☐	Bisque Tortoni	☐	
Cocoanut	☐	Mocha Walnut	☐	
Chocolate Chip	☐	Swiss Chocolate Almond	☐	
Black Raspberry	☐	Orange Sherbet	☐	
Peach	☐	Tangerine Sherbet	☐	
Peppermint Stick	☐	Pineapple Sherbet	☐	
Caramel Fudge	☐	Lemon Sherbet	☐	
Burgundy Cherry	☐	Raspberry Sherbet	☐	
Mocha Chip	☐	Lime Sherbet	☐	
_____	☐	_____	☐	
_____	☐	_____	☐	
_____	☐	_____	☐	

Ask Mom and Dad to Stop at a

HOWARD JOHNSON'S

MOTOR LODGE

When Traveling

In an effort to encourage return visits, Howard Johnson's printed the "Ice Cream Game" on the back of the children's menu. *Courtesy of Tony Abbott.*

went to HoJo's after church on Sundays. I remember weekends being a big deal with families coming in." Wilson said that the all-you-can-eat nights attracted many customers. "The fish fries on Fridays were a big deal," she said. "All-you-can-eat clams were on Wednesdays, and at one time, Tuesdays were all-you-can-eat spaghetti." Wilson remembers one of the most frequently ordered menu items was the hot dog on a buttered, toasted roll served with baked beans and Boston brown bread.

But HoJo's wasn't just for families. "There were a lot of influential people who used to come in," said Wilson. "One person I remember in particular who was a regular we used to call old man Burr. It was William Burr from the Burr family." The Burrs were one of the original families to settle in Fairfield. "He used to come in almost every day; he would sit at the counter and order a sandwich. I loved it when I got to work the counter. That's where you heard all the gossip as one person would talk to another."

The only problem with working the counter, Wilson said, was that you got all sticky from handling all the ice cream.

The restaurant almost met its demise in 1962 when a fire

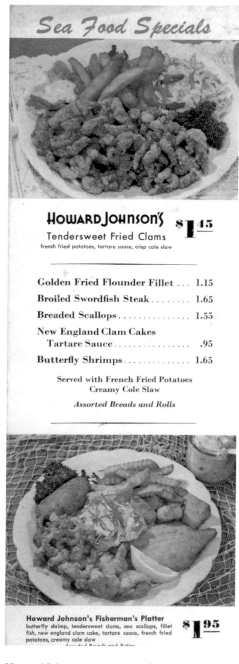

Howard Johnson's was known for its fried clam dinners. *Courtesy of Sue Steele.*

sandwiches

HOWARD JOHNSON'S GRILLED FRANKFORT on Toasted Roll	.30
BARBECUED SLICED BEEF on Toasted Roll	.60
AMERICAN CHEESE .35 Grilled	.40
BACON, LETTUCE AND TOMATO	.60
WESTERN — Roll or Sandwich	.55
BAKED HAM .55 With Cheese	.65
TUNA FISH — Salad on Finger Roll	.55
SLICED TURKEY	.85
HAM SALAD	.45

hamburger specialties

QUARTER POUND HAMBURG Toasted Roll .60 With Smothered Onions	.65
GRILLED HAMBURG STEAK Toasted Roll .40 With Smothered Onions	.45
CHEESEBURGER on Toasted Roll	.50
GRILLED HAMBURG, Toasted Roll French Fried Potatoes, Cole Slaw	.85
CHEESEBURGER on Toasted Roll French Fried Potatoes, Cole Slaw	.95

Ho-Jo's 3-D

3 GIANT DECKS OF THE MOST
DELICIOUS EATIN' EVER WITH 3-D SAUCE

King of all the Cheeseburgers! 75¢

With French Fried Potatoes, Cole Slaw 1.15

hot sandwiches

TENDERSWEET CLAM ROLL, Tartare Sauce	.75
With French Fried Potatoes, Cole Slaw	1.10
BARBECUED SLICED BEEF, Toasted Roll French Fried Potatoes, Cole Slaw	.95
HOT BEEF SANDWICH, Brown Gravy French Fried Potatoes	1.20
OPEN STEAK SANDWICH French Fried Potatoes, Cole Slaw	1.35

OPEN HOT ROAST TURKEY SANDWICH Homestyle Dressing, Giblet Gravy French Fried Potatoes, Cranberry Sauce ... 1.30

triple decker sandwiches

#1 SLICED TURKEY, GRILLED BACON SLICED TOMATO, Crisp Lettuce Mayonnaise, Potato Chips	1.25
#2 BAKED HAM, CHEESE, Dill Pickles Crisp Lettuce, Mayonnaise, Potato Chips	.95
#3 TUNA FISH, EGG SALAD, LETTUCE and TOMATO, Mayonnaise, Potato Chips	.95

DR-200-K

For only seventy-five cents, diners could order the King of All Cheeseburgers, complete with 3-D sauce. *Courtesy of Sue Steele.*

broke out in the kitchen.[158] It was a Saturday night, and the dining room was packed. Forty-eight members of Hofstra University's football squad were celebrating their victory against the University of Bridgeport a few hours earlier when the manager quietly asked them to leave. As it turned out, the grease duct in the kitchen was overtaxed and a fire ignited, spreading through the area beneath the roof. Two fire companies arrived at the scene and were able to extinguish the fire. The damage was estimated at more than $20,000, and the restaurant was closed for a few weeks. It reopened, however, and remained a popular spot for four decades. The Fairfield Howard Johnson's served its last ice cream cone right after the Memorial Day parade in 1996.

On the Southport end of town, the Farm Shop was the place to go after shopping at nearby Barkers. The lunch and dinner menus offered a variety of options. There were cheeseburgers and egg salad with lettuce and tomato, but also date nut bread and cream cheese sandwiches and the "Fridayburger," a nod to the Catholic community: a golden fried fish patty with melted cheese and coleslaw.[159]

LUNCH OR DINNER

LITTLE BOY BLUE

Grilled Hamburger Patty, Mashed Potato, Fresh Vegetable, Roll and Butter, Ice Cream and Cake Square **90c**

SMALL FRY

Howard Johnson's Tendersweet Fried Clams with Potato, Roll and Butter, Ice Cream, Sherbet or Gelatine. **95c**

MISS MUFFET LUNCH

Petite Fresh Vegetable Plate, Bacon Strip, Roll and Butter, Ice Cream, Sherbet or Gelatine. **75c**

JACK HORNER LUNCH

Peanut Butter & Jelly Sandwich, Ice Cream, Sherbet, Cake or Gelatine. **55c**

THE FISHERMAN

Golden Brown Fish Fillet, Mashed Potatoes, Fresh Vegetable, Buttered Toast Triangles, Ice Cream, Sherbet or Gelatine. **85c**

TOMMY TUCKER PLATE

Sliced Roast Turkey, Fresh Vegetable, Mashed Potato and Gravy, Roll and Butter, Ice Cream, Sherbet, Cake or Gelatine. **1 00**

HUMPTY DUMPTY

Small Tuna Fish Salad on Crisp Lettuce, Tomato and Potato Chip Garnish, Roll and Butter, Ice Cream, Sherbet or Gelatine. **95c**

SIMPLE SIMON SPECIAL

Roast Beef, Gravy, Fresh Vegetable and Potato, Roll and Butter, Ice Cream, Sherbet or Gelatine. **1 10**

Choice of MILK, CHOCOLATE MILK, HOT CHOCOLATE, ORANGE DRINK

For Your Convenience—Strained Baby Foods . . . 25c

BREAKFAST WITH SIMPLE SIMON

FROM MOTHER HUBBARD'S CUPBOARD	THREE BEARS BAIT	JACK SPRATT'S PLATE	MRS. SPRATT'S PLATE
Chilled Orange Juice, Short Stack of Hot Cakes, Whipped Butter—Warm Syrup, Chocolate or Plain Milk **60c**	Orange Juice, Cooked or Dry Cereal with Fresh Milk, Buttered Toast Slice, Choc. or Plain Milk **55c**	Orange Juice, Poached Egg on Toast, Chocolate or Plain Milk **55c**	Orange Juice, Boiled or Poached Egg in a Cup, Strip of Crisp Bacon, Buttered Toast Slice, Chocolate or Plain Milk **60c**

Before the invention of chicken nuggets, the Howard Johnson's children's menu included the Miss Muffet lunch, consisting of vegetables, bacon and a roll with butter. *Courtesy of Tony Abbott.*

For those feeling particularly festive, there was the Silver Platter for Two: a sandwich variety platter including ham, turkey, bacon, lettuce, cottage cheese, coleslaw, tomato, stuffed olives and French fried potatoes attractively served on a silver platter. According to the menu, it was plenty for two hearty appetites (or one big one).

As tempting as the Silver Platter for Two may have been, those watching their waistlines could instead order the Health Salad Plate, which consisted of cottage cheese on peach halves and shredded lettuce with strawberry dressing and rye bread.

But of course, the real reason everyone went to the Farm Shop was to indulge in the ice cream. The flavor list rivaled that of Howard Johnson's (and, in fact, was practically the same). But their sundaes were one of a kind. Take, for example, the Stupendous, Incompressible Serendipity Sundae. The menu description says, "15 flavors of ice cream, 8 kinds of topping, 3 bananas, whipped cream, candy sprinkles, etc. etc." Or the Certificate Sundae with its three large heaps of ice cream and a cup of hot fudge. If the customer finished the entire sundae, they were awarded a certificate. But by far the most popular was the Abigail Super Sundae: seven flavors of ice cream, five toppings, clouds of whipped cream, candy garnish and "two spoons if needed."

Theresa McGrath remembers working at the Farm Shop as a waitress from 1976 to 1978. "We wore white dresses and nurse's shoes," she said. "Once I was on a train and some old man laid down and said 'Help me.' He thought I was a nurse."[160]

Eventually, the Farm Shop closed, and in 1987, it became a Friendly's, which remained open until 2011.

Allington's, located at 70 Reef Road, was known for its old-fashioned ice cream parlor atmosphere. There were round marble tables with vintage-style iron chairs. Soups and sandwiches were on the menu, but the homemade ice cream was the star. Flavors would change every day, but the restaurant's chocolate lace ice cream—bits of dark chocolate–covered lacey brittle mixed into vanilla ice cream—was the signature flavor. In 1988, Timothy's took over the spot. Serving homemade ice cream, Timothy's (owned by Timothy Larkin) was a fixture in Black Rock and had opened a second location in Shelton. Fairfield was the third. Melissa Stewart worked at Timothy's in the summers when she was home from college. "That place was non-stop," she said. "If there was a concert on the green, there would be a line out the door for three to four hours." The big draw were the "mix-ins"—bits of candy, cookies and brownies were mixed into ice cream on a marble slab using paddles. "We had to make sure the customer saw us mixing it in. All the ice cream was made by Tim," she said. "He switched flavors weekly. He would make certain special flavors, like Sweet Cream." The flavor signs were all hand-drawn and changed daily according to what was available. There were specialty flavors like banana sorbet, Black Rock (vanilla with chocolate-covered almonds), mocha and peppermint and everyday favorites like French vanilla, sweet cream, Dutch chocolate, Oreo, strawberry, chocolate chip and coffee. Stewart recalled making ice cream cakes from scratch. "We'd grind up Oreos or graham crackers as the base and then layer ice cream in a springform pan. If it rained, you literally made cakes all day." Sundays were spent making edible bowls out of waffles. "Tim really was an ice cream visionary," said Stewart. "No one had those things then. It was really important the customer was happy. He was really nice but no joke, ice cream was his passion." The Fairfield location closed in 1995 due to a lease dispute, but the Black Rock location has thrived for over thirty years.

14

ꝹAST CALL

Creating a New Culinary History

Fairfield's culinary landscape has grown and changed tremendously over the years. The town that started off with a handful of taverns and ordinaries is the same place that today offers a huge range of dining options. In the 1970s and '80s, Fairfield began to see more chain restaurants like Arthur Treacher's, Bonanza and Pizzeria Uno move in. These family-friendly dining establishments altered the entire dining out experience. Restaurant going, which had once been an occasional treat, was now a regular, oftentimes weekly, occurrence.

In 1975, a book called *Fairfield County: An Insider's Guide* was published. In chapter four, "Where Should We Eat Tonight?," the author preps us with this intro:

> *It's necessary to start this chapter with a cautionary note. Fairfield County is not, in general, a famous gastronomic center. Its restaurants do not and cannot be expected to compare with New York City's for variety, excitement or even, in most cases, the quality of the cooking. However, it is possible to eat well in a number of restaurants and there certainly are others which provide satisfactory escape from the routine of home cooking.* [161]

My, how times have changed. First of all, zoning regulations were loosened so that it became much easier for restaurants to open in town. The 1,500-foot rule no longer exists, and the Post Road is a virtual treasure trove of restaurant options, from casual dining to sophisticated al fresco

When chain restaurants started to open in Fairfield, Bonanza was one of the most popular. *Courtesy of Susan Dombrowski.*

cafés. With so much competition, the restaurants in Fairfield have to be good. There's no room for mediocrity when one can simply choose to go to another restaurant just a few doors away. Today, Fairfield County ranks number two nationally in the top metro areas for eating out. According to Trulia, a real estate website, this area is second only to San Francisco for per capita density of restaurants. In Fairfield County, there are 27.6 restaurants per ten thousand households.[162]

Secondly, New York's gastronomic influence has certainly spread to the suburbs. Celebrity chefs live and work here. Yes, self-taught cooks do run many restaurants in town, but there are just as many Le Cordon Bleu–trained, Escoffier-style, James Beard Award–winning chefs creating amazing menus in the suburbs.

When chain restaurants started to arrive in town, Arthur Treacher's was one of the first to arrive in Southport. *Courtesy of Susan Dombrowski.*

So where should we dine tonight? The world is your oyster (or clam or mussel) in Fairfield. Whether you're looking for pizza by the slice or a fancy steak-and-red-wine dinner, there are plenty of options in this New York City suburb. Every new restaurant, every chef and waiter, is part of a new narrative that we are creating now. So save your menus and share your stories. It's all history in the making.

Notes

Chapter 1

1. Mary Darlington Taylor, "Colonial Tavern Vied in Importance with Meetin' House," *Bridgeport (CT) Sunday Post*, August 16, 1935.
2. Fairfield Museum and History Center archives.
3. William Lee, "Samuel Penfield House: Sun Tavern," Report, Fairfield Museum and History Center.
4. Helen Harrison, "Historic Houses: Historic Sun Tavern," Fairfield Museum and History Center.
5. Ibid.
6. Taylor, "Colonial Tavern Vied."
7. Marian Dickinson Terry, *Old Inns of Connecticut* (Hartford, CT: Prospect Press, 1937).
8. Taylor, "Colonial Tavern Vied."
9. Terry, *Old Inns of Connecticut*.
10. Elizabeth Banks MacRury, *More About the Hill—Greenfield Hill* (New Haven, CT: City Printing Co.,1968).
11. Thomas J. Farnham, *Fairfield: The Biography of a Community, 1639–1989* (West Kennebunk, ME: Phoenix Publishing, 1989), 105.
12. MacRury, *More About the Hill*.
13. Ibid.

Chapter 2

14. Elizabeth Hubbell Schenck, *The History of Fairfield, Fairfield County, Connecticut from the Settlement of the Town in 1639 to 1818* (self-published, 1889).

15. Fairfield Temperance Society papers, Voluntary Associations Collection, Fairfield Museum and History Center.

16. Farnham, *Fairfield: Biography of a Community*, 159.

17. Edward James Speer, *Pequot the Village School: 50 Years* (Ann Arbor, MI: Edward Brothers Inc., 1967).

18. *Bridgeport (CT) Evening Farmer*, November 9, 1911.

19. Ibid., November 11, 1911.

20. Ibid., July 1, 1911.

21. Ibid., January 16, 1913.

22. "Lays Out Seven Disputants with Aid of Crowbar," *Bridgeport (CT) Evening Farmer*, September 19, 1916.

23. Ibid.

24. *Bridgeport (CT) Evening Farmer*, June 28, 1915.

25. Ibid., July 6, 1915.

26. One has to wonder if his campaign slogan was "Everyone loves Bacon!"

27. Farnham, *Fairfield: Biography of a Community*, 235.

28. "Widening of Pequot Ave. and Remodeling of James Building: 1947–48," *Southport Packet* 3, no. 1 (January 1989).

29. John B. Payne, "Tales of Boyhood Days," *Southport Packet* 3, no. 3 (July 1989).

30. "Widening of Pequot Ave.," *Southport Packet*.

31. Robert Adams, "Plan to Let Bars Down Stirs Booze Men, WCTU," *Connecticut Sunday Herald*, April 1, 1962.

32. Interview with Christine Sismondo, June 10, 2015.

33. John Koziol, "New and Improved: Al's Place Café Sporting New Look, New Outlook," *Fairfield (CT) Citizen News*, January 29, 1999.

34. Andrew Brophy, "Patrons Toast Fairfield Bar as It Shuts Its Doors," *Connecticut Post*, June 2006.

35. Michael J. Daly, "End of 'The Drift' Marks the End of an Era," *Connecticut Post*, June 25, 2006.

36. Andrew Brophy, "Fairfield Losing Another Tavern," *Connecticut Post*, June 22, 2006.

37. Interview with Joseph Sepot, February 2015.

38. *Bridgeport (CT) Post*, August 30, 1975.

39. Ibid.

40. Interview with Jen Collison, August 2, 2015.

41. Interview with Mary Beth Ross, August 2, 2015.

42. Cindy Simoneau and Robert Fredericks, "Court Shuts Popular Tavern," *Bridgeport (CT) Post*, December 4, 1985.

43. Interview with Ellie Simpson, May 8, 2015.

44. Interview with John Barnhart, June 2, 2015.

45. Henry Fountain, "Taverns Not Tapped Out by Changing Times," *Fairfield (CT) Citizen News*, February 16, 1983.

46. *Bridgeport (CT) Telegram*, March 27, 1951.

47. Andrew Brophy, "Owner Hopes to Revive Tony D's," *Connecticut Post*, November 18, 2002.

CHAPTER 3

48. Jan Whitaker, "At the Sign of the…" *Restaurant-ing Through History*, January 21, 2015, http://restaurant-ingthroughhistory.com/2015/01/21/at-the-sign-of-the.
49. "Mrs. Henry S. Glover's Tea for Her Guest Proves to Be Delightful Affair," June 16, 1915, clipping from the Fairfield Museum and History Center.
50. Ibid.
51. Mrs. William Boyd, "History of the Old Academy Tea Room," December 11, 1979, clipping from the Fairfield Museum and History Center.
52. Ibid.
53. "Mrs. Henry S. Glover's Tea," June 16, 1915.
54. Ibid.
55. Ibid.
56. Ibid.
57. Boyd, "History of the S."
58. Carolyn Morgan, "Topics of the Town," clipping from the Fairfield Museum and History Center.
59. Clipping from the Fairfield Museum and History Center.
60. "Visiting Nurses' Greenfield Lawn Party Successful," *Bridgeport (CT) Evening Farmer*, July 1, 1915.
61. Ibid.
62. Brochure in the collections of the Fairfield Museum and History Center.
63. "Slouch Hatted Culprits Busy in Fairfield," *Bridgeport (CT) Evening Farmer*, July 7, 1916.
64. MacRury, *More About the Hill*.
65. Ibid.
66. Ibid.
67. Ibid.
68. *Bridgeport (CT) Evening Farmer*, July 1, 1915.
69. Ibid.
70. MacRury, *More About the Hill*.

CHAPTER 4

71. Interview with Beth Bilyard, August 27, 2015.
72. Christopher B. Nevins, "The Southport Tide Mill Has at Least 'Nine' Lives," *Southport Packet* 1, no. 4 (October 1987).
73. Ibid.
74. Ibid.
75. John B. Payne, "The Tide Mill Tavern," *Southport Packet* 1, no. 4 (October 1987).
76. Ibid.
77. Interview with Christopher Rountos, May 2015.
78. "Redding Ridge, Connecticut, History, Past and Present," History of Redding, http://www.historyofredding.com/HRreddingridge.htm.
79. Payne, "Tide Mill Tavern."

80. *Redding (CT) Times*, September 12, 1957.

81. *Bridgeport (CT) Telegram*, April 29, 1954.

82. Thanks to Christopher Rountos, current owner of the Spinning Wheel Inn, who made available his copy of the out-of-print book.

83. Lucia J. Parks, "The Pequot Inn," *Southport Packet* 11, no. 1 (January 1997).

84. *Fairfield (CT) News*, September 1953.

Chapter 5

85. "'Gas Light Era' Revived at Center Restaurant," *Bridgeport (CT) Sunday Post*, September 6, 1959.

86. Interview with Tom Papageorge, May 2015.

87. "'Gas Light Era' Revived," *Bridgeport (CT) Sunday Post*.

88. "Dinner with Cocktail $1.25 in Fairfield Eatery Event," *Bridgeport (CT) Telegram*, September 4, 1962.

89. Interview with Maureen Delaney, June 2015.

Chapter 6

90. Mary K. Witkowski, "Musician Owned Shop, Eatery," *Bridgeport (CT) News*, September 6, 2007.

91. Interview with Susan Burke.

92. Interview with Jerry Buswell.

93. "Ratzenberger's 'Continental' Opens, Specializes in Hungarian Cuisine," *Bridgeport (CT) Post*, May 2, 1954.

94. Interview with Joann Dos Santos.

95. Interview with Bob Delancy, June 2, 2015.

96. Patty Malkin, "Dining Out," *Connecticut Sunday Herald*, 1972.

97. Interview with Howard Meyer, February 2015.

98. Graham, "Dining Out with Barbara Graham," *Connecticut Sunday Herald*, October 20, 1963.

99. "William A. Ratzenberger, Musician, Restaurateur dies," *Fairfield (CT) Citizen News*, October 7, 1983.

100. "Millie Ratzenberger Manning," Findagrave.com, http://www.findagrave.com/cgi-bin/fg.cgi?page=gr&GRid=45791302.

Chapter 7

101. *Bridgeport (CT) Sunday Post*, January 2, 1955.

102. "Jerry O'Mahony Dining Cars," Federal Lounge, http://www.thefedoralounge.com/showthread.php?36808-c-1943-O-Mahony-diner-catalogue-%28complete%29.

103. Nancy P. Serrell, "Larry's Diner: Local Landmark to Say Goodbye," *Fairfield (CT) Citizen News*, October 9, 1985.

104. Charles C. Kadar obituary, *Connecticut Post*, February 6, 2003.

105. "Diner: Larry's Dishes Up Art Deco as New Restaurant's Centerpiece," *New Haven (CT) Register*, April 3, 1988.

106. Harry Neigher, *Connecticut Sunday Herald*, February 17, 1963.

107. "Stergios Koutikas obituary," Obitsforlife.com, http://obitsforlife.com/obituary/336111/Koutikas-Stergios.php.

108. "Bertha Erdoss obituary," Obitsforlife.com, http://www.legacy.com/obituaries/ctpost/obituary.aspx?pid=172461267.

109. "Elsie Byrd obituary," Riverview Funeral Home, http://riverviewfh.com/obituary.php?w=1433

110. Andrew Brophy, "Vegging Out: Diner Breaks Tradition with Vegetarian Fare," *Fairfield (CT) Minuteman*, December 5, 1996.

111. Rick Green and Lisa Chedekel, "Bridgeport Corruption Scandal: City's Miracle Comes Under a Cloud," *Hartford (CT) Courant*, June 17, 2001.

112. Andrew Brophy, "After 63 Years, Diner Is Done," *Connecticut Post*, September 27, 2005.

Chapter 8

113. Interview with Kuhn family, May 26, 2015.

114. C.B. Cebulski, "The Best Thing I Ever Ate—at the Deli," *Eatak*, http://www.eataku.com/post/1356727184/best-thing-i-ever-ate-at-the-deli.

Chapter 9

115. Graham, "Dining Out with Barbara Graham," *Connecticut Sunday Herald*, November 25, 1962.

116. Graham, "Dining Out with Barbara Graham," *Connecticut Sunday Herald*, December 15, 1963.

117. Interview with Otto Veglio, July 2015.

118. "Cocktails Open Fairfield's New Catering Firm," *Bridgeport (CT) Telegram*, May 28, 1973.

119. Interview with Tony Danforth.

120. Interview with Lewis Chappell.

121. Interview with Melanie Stewart.

Chapter 10

122. Interview with Howard Meyer.

123. Joe Satran, "Credit Cards and Restaurants: Industries Mull 'Cashless' Dining Consequences," January 23, 2013, http://www.huffingtonpost.com/2013/01/23/credit-cards-restaurants-cashless-dining_n_2482242.html.

124. Lois M. Plunkert, "The 1980's: A Decade of Job Growth and Industry Shift," *Monthly Labor Review*, September 1990, http://www.bls.gov/mlr/1990/09/art1full.pdf.

125. Patti Woods, "Not Tucker-ed Out After 2 Decades," June 6, 2011, *Fairfield (CT) Citizen,* http://www.fairfieldcitizenonline.com/news/article/EatDrinkShopCook-Not-Tucker-ed-out-after-2-1410349.php.

126. Cindy Clarke, "22 Years Strong: Tucker's Café Is Still Cozy After All These Years," *Fairfield (CT) Minuteman,* November 22, 2011.

CHAPTER 11

127. Interview with Thomas Febbraio, February 2015.

128. Interview with Ed Waiksnis, February 2015.

129. Bill Bittar, "Tommy's Restaurant Changes Hands After 25 Years," *Fairfield (CT) Minuteman,* February 6, 2003.

130. *Fairfield (CT) Citizen News,* July 19, 1978.

131. Interview with Joseph Sepot, February 2015.

132. Jill Amadio, "It's Greek Easter—Visit Acropolis," *Connecticut Sunday Herald,* April 29, 1973.

133. Douglas Clement, "In Fairfield, Breakaway Does Fish, and Everything Else, in Its Own Special Way," *Fairfield County Times Monthly,* July 1997.

CHAPTER 12

134. *Bridgeport (CT) Evening Farmer,* August 10, 1911.

135. Ibid., July 25, 1913.

136. Ibid., February 17, 1911.

137. Patti Woods, "No Need for Nostalgia: Devore's Is Back!" May 16, 2010, *Fairfield (CT) Patch,* http://patch.com/connecticut/fairfield/no-need-for-nostalgia-devores-is-back.

138. Interview with Rosemarie Corr, February 25, 2015.

139. Interview with Carol Black, February 25, 2015.

140. Interview with Linda Malkin, February 25, 2015.

141. Interview with Jonathan Chernes, February 25, 2015.

142. Interview with Dolores Abbott, February 25, 2015.

143. Interview with Jessie Murphy, February 25, 2015.

144. "A Local Favorite 75 Years in the Baking: Devore's, a Post Road Gem, Marks Its Diamond Anniversary," *Fairfield (CT) Minuteman,* July 20, 1995.

145. "Devore's Bakery Files Bankruptcy, Stays Open," *Fairfield (CT) Minuteman,* July 16, 1998.

146. "Devore's Adds Delicatessen," *Fairfield (CT) Citizen News,* April 1, 2005.

147. "Local Bakery No Match for National Advertisers," *Connecticut Post,* May 3, 2006.

148. Woods, "No Need for Nostalgia."

149. Submitted by Stephen Skutel.

150. Interview with Elizabeth Van De Bogart, August 3, 2015.

151. Interview with Art Green, February 2015.

152. Interview with Beth Herde, February 2015.

153. Interview with Patricia Nichols, July 31, 2015.

154. Andrew Brophy, "Pie Plate Sets Interim Return for a Slice of Holiday Trade," *Fairfield (CT) Minuteman*, November 14, 1996.

CHAPTER 13

155. Lolita Baldor, "Buddy's—Old-fashioned Seaside Treat," *Fairfield (CT) Citizen News*, June 3, 1983.

156. Farnham, *Fairfield: Biography of a Community*, 200.

157. Interview with Brenda Wilson, July 23, 2015.

158. "Fairfield Eatery Fire Routs Grid Squad at Victory Fete," *Bridgeport (CT) Telegram*, October 15, 1962.

159. Menu courtesy of Charlie Crowell.

160. Interview with Theresa McGrath, March 24, 2015.

CHAPTER 14

161. Parke Cummings and Nora Lapin, *Fairfield County: An Insider's Guide* (New York: Lawrence Hill and Company, 1975).

162. Jed Kolko, "Eating Towns, Drinking Towns," *Trulia*, http://www.trulia.com/trends/2012/08/eating-towns-drinking-towns.

9NDEX

INDEX

W

Wakeman, Bacon 17, 18
Willowby's 86

Y

Your Brother's Suspenders 27

ABOUT THE AUTHOR

Patti Woods grew up in Fairfield, where she lived for over twenty-five years. She is the former Good Living editor for the *Fairfield* and *Westport Minuteman* newspapers and writer of the "EatDrinkShopCook" column for the *Fairfield Citizen* and *Westport News*. She's the former managing editor of *Better Nutrition* magazine and has won numerous awards for her feature writing. Patti has been freelancing for fifteen years, writing for magazines such as *Wine Spectator*, *Health* and *Delicious Living*. Although she still mourns the loss of Sidetracks and Breakaway, she is passionate about discovering new restaurants in Fairfield and surrounding towns. Patti lives in Trumbull, Connecticut, with her husband and son.

Photo by Nick Gamma.